Progressing in English ©

The Adventures of the Pasquati Family©

The Pasquatis Plan to Go to Scotland ©

This the second edition (2021).

It has been revised and expanded with more exercises and grammar.

Campbell McPherson M.A., B.A., Post Graduate Certificate in Education, Post Graduate Certificate in Teaching English as a Foreign Language.

Campbell taught English as a Foreign Language and English for Special and Academic Purposes in British universities and colleges for some 30 years.

Acknowledgements

My sincere thanks to the following for their help and useful comments in developing *The Pasquatis Plan to Go to Scotland* :

Emeritus Professor M. Mozzon McPherson (England)

Mr Dimitri Spelta (Italy)

Dr. E. Arvanitaki (Greece)

Dott.ssa A. Trevisson-Hoyler (Germany)

Any errors remain mine.

Introduction

Progressing in English© *The Pasquatis Plan to Go to Scotland* © is intended to provide a stimulating approach to improving language skills, especially in reading, comprehension and grammar.

The intention is that the content will allow users to work independently. The texts are suitable for learners with an upper-intermediate/intermediate knowledge of British English. The language and grammar will progressively* become more difficult.

Progressively is used here to mean *with the passage of time, as you progress [move through] the work.*

Because the language used is current, the publication is also of value to those who wish to update their knowledge of British English as it is used in the 2020s.

The adventures of the Pasquati family are used as a framework, a central theme, divided into episodes. The hope is that readers will find the story interesting and benefit by:

* Increasing vocabulary,

* Improving analytical reading and skills in English,

* Understand the grammar used and developing the ability to manipulate language,

* Increasing knowledge of the UK, including its culture and history.

The **Answers** to the exercises are contained at the end of each section.

Tricky Questions

Internationally, some examinations, university entrance tests, and school tests use **True, False** and **Not Given.**

It is therefore important to read both the text and questions carefully and to identify which information is **Not Given.**

I have included some **Not Given** questions **[TRICKY QUESTIONS]** to help you practise this useful skill.

Constructive comments and suggestions are welcome. **Email:** familypasquati@gmail.com

Episode One

Origins

The Pasquatis lived on the top floor of a block of flats in a small town, south of Rimini on the Adriatic coast. From their balcony they could easily get a clear view over the sea, the neighbours were quiet and friendly, and the family's only complaint was the tendency for the lift to breakdown on an increasingly frequent basis.

Mr. Pasquati thought that the lift needed to be replaced. It was over thirty years old according to the manufacturer's plate on the floor, and Mr. Pasquati had a degree and background in engineering. He was actually the owner of a small engineering company, which he had inherited from his father and expanded to produce a wider range of products of improved quality. The company had been doing well until the European recession, and increasing competition from China, had started to reduce its profits.

Mrs. Pasquati had been a product designer when she met her husband at a trade fair, but had only worked **part**-time since the birth of their first child and now felt that many of her skills were out-of-date. They had now been married for some twenty years and had two children. Their daughter, Francesca, was seventeen and still at school. She had a passion for both art and the outdoors, while her older brother Pietro, who had done very well at school, seemed to have developed only a passion for drinking and chasing girls rather than his university classes. Francesca regularly told her Mum that she thought Pietro was *a total loser* and the two regularly squabbled (1) over even minor things. Pietro thought that Francesca was old for her age (2) and regularly warned her to stop being so critical.

The Pasquatis had first met (3) the MacDonalds, a Scottish family, years earlier when Peter and Helen went to Italy with their parents for a holiday. They were staying (4) in the same hotel near the beach, and the Scottish children started playing with Francesca and Pietro both on the beach and in the hotel when the midday sun was too hot. They were roughly the same age, Pietro being the oldest of the group by a year, and shared some interests. Both the boys liked football, though Scottish football was a mystery to Pietro who had only heard of clubs from Liverpool and Manchester. Francesca and Helen both loved music and dancing.

Over the years, the two families had often shared summer holidays together. Sometimes they met in Italy, but after a while the Scots got (5) bored of returning to the same hotel and place, and finally managed to persuade their friends to either go to different Italian regions or try Greece or other Mediterranean countries. Going somewhere hot was an essential part of any arrangement, though the Scottish family became increasingly cautious about the midday sun after Mrs. MacDonald had a severe (6) case of sunstroke and spent (7) almost a week in hospital on a small Greek island. The following year, the Italians decided to visit Scotland.

Language Notes

(1) **Squabbled.** Squabble is an interesting word. It is often used to describe the daily arguments between young children and so has a lower status than the word *argument*. However, it can also be used to describe something more serious and potentially dangerous, such as an argument between countries over a border, but in such a case the word is used to indicate that the behaviour of those involved is not very mature – *childish* effectively.

(2) **Old for her age.** She was behaving like someone much older.

(3) Note the use of the past perfect here. Many people would use the past simple (*The four first met)* and in modern English this is generally acceptable.

The relationship between the past simple and the past perfect becomes more important when certainty is required. Think about the difference between *He forgot their wedding anniversary and his wife left him.* and *He had forgotten their wedding anniversary and his wife left him.* The second sentence suggests a strong link between the fact that *he had forgotten* and the decision by his wife to leave him.

(4) **They had been staying** is an alternative, but the original sentence is already clear.

(5) English is full of verbal structures using **to get.** *Get to. Get to know. Get round to doing something. To get over. To get into* etc.

Some have multiple meanings. So, *To get over a river* is geographical movement but *To get over a relationship* is to recover from the sadness resulting from a failed relationship.

You will learn all the terms and their meanings with experience, but the general rule is **DO NOT FILL YOUR SENTENCES WITH 'GETS'.**

(6) **Severe** means <u>bad</u> in this context.

(7) **Spent** Here spent is used to describe a passage of time. *E.g. He spent nearly ten years in the army.*

Back home in Scotland, the MacDonalds might have told their friends that *Mrs. MacDonald ended up in hospital* or that *she landed [up]* in hospital.*

* Both are possible. These are both commonly used terms -despite the fact that Mrs MacDonald is not an aircraft! In more formal English *she was admitted to hospital.*

Grammar Note

This first section uses the *Past Simple* and other past tenses *The Pasquatis lived on the top floor of a block of flats.*

The Past Simple is **usually used** to describe a **finished act** in the past as in the schematic below. **There is normally a fixed time associated with the Past Simple.**

For example [E.g.]

I **met** Helen in the summer of **2012.**

Bill **left** school in **2015** and **immediately joined** the navy.

We **went** for a meal in the local restaurant **last night** and **ate** a very good meal.

But in stories and narratives you will see that this sense of time is **not so essential and is sometimes partially or totally lost.**

E.g. *We met one hot summer and married soon after. It was love at first sight and I was always happy with the choice I made that lovely summer's day.*

IF YOU ARE UNSURE, KEEP TO THE RULE – PAST SIMPLE NEEDS A PRECISE TIME.

Past Simple

X

Past   Event   With Time   **Now**

Comprehension

1. Which of these statements best describes the lift in the Pasquati's building?

a) The lift was always broken.
b) The lift broke down with increasing regularity.
c) The lift broke down regularly.
d) There was a plate on the floor which said that it needed to be replaced.

2. From the Pasquati's balcony they could easily see the sea. Therefore, the balcony could not have been facing in which direction? *(Use the Internet or a map of Italy for this if you need to).*

3. Which one word best replaces *roughly* in the context of this sentence?

4. Which of the following **most fully** justifies Mr. Pasquati's conclusion that the lift should be replaced?

a) His degree was in engineering and the lift kept breaking down.

b) The manufacturers said that it was too old and unreliable.

c) Mr Pasquati had a degree in engineering, had practical engineering experience, knew the age of the lift and found it unreliable.

d) Mr Pasquati had a degree in engineering, had practical engineering experience and knew the age of the lift.

5. *Scottish football was a mystery to Pietro.* In your own words, explain why this might be the case.

What do you think of the use of the word **mystery**?

What difference would it make if the sentence had been written to say *Pietro was ignorant of Scottish football?*

6. Mrs MacDonald had a severe case of sunstroke. In English, write a list of her possible symptoms. (*Use the Internet or reliable sources for this.*)

Some Past Simple Work for You

Where are the mistakes in these sentences? There are 9.

When I was young I went to a good school, but my course at university were very disappointing. After two years I leaved the university and applied for a job in a government agency.

I work there for two years and then I received a promotion, but I were still very bored and after another year I resigned and returned to university to study a different subject. I was over 20 then, and have a wife but no children. My wife was very understanding and help me with my studies. When I finished my first degree, she encourage me to continue my studies, and she supported me by working part-time in a local school. Finally, I obtained my doctorate and a post as a professor in a good university. A year later we decide to start a family and our son arrive the following year.

Crossword (There are some links to the story so far).

Clues
Across

4. The violent opposite of 12.   **6.** Not happy, so I'm going to do something
7. It goes up and down   **9.** Kicking a round thing around
11. Several of a similar type   **12.** Pick up

Down

1. At 12   **2.** Being careful
3. Dark at 12. Opposite of 1.   **5.** Put a cover on it to reduce cooking time.
8. Like very much-perhaps to marry?
10. Ask a friend to take you somewhere by transport (To give you a xxxx)

ANSWERS

1. **b)** The lift broke down with increasing regularity.
2. It would be impossible to see westwards from the balcony. The Adriatic Sea is to the east of Italy.
3. Approximately
4. **c)** Mr Pasquati had a degree in engineering, had practical engineering experience, knew the age of the lift and found it unreliable.
5. Scottish football does not receive much attention in the international media. *Mystery* is often used to describe something which is difficult to understand or about which there is no or little knowledge.

An example: *It's a mystery why he bought that car. It's always in the garage and the repairs cost a fortune.*

ignorant of Scottish football. It's normally very rude to say that someone is ignorant.

6. **Some** symptoms of sunstroke include:

A high temperature	Headache	Feeling thirsty
Feeling very hot	Nausea and vomiting	Fast pulse
Being agitated/ confused /disorientated		Having a drop in blood pressure
Rapid, shallow breathing		Losing consciousness / fainting

Answers Some Past Simple Work for You

When I was young I went to a good school, but my course at university WAS very disappointing. After two years I *LEFT** the university and applied for a job in a government agency.

I WORKED there for two years and then I received a promotion, but I *WAS** still very bored and after another year I resigned and returned to university to study a different subject. I was over 20 then, and HAD a wife but no children. My wife was very understanding and HELPED me with my studies. When I finished my first degree, she ENCOURAGED me to continue my studies and she supported me by working part-time in a local school. Finally, I obtained my doctorate and a post as a professor in a good university. A year later we DECIDED to start a family and our son ARRIVED the following year.

*Irregular Verbs to Remember

Infinitive	Past Simple	Past Participle
To go	went	gone
To leave	left	left
To be	was	been

Crossword Answers

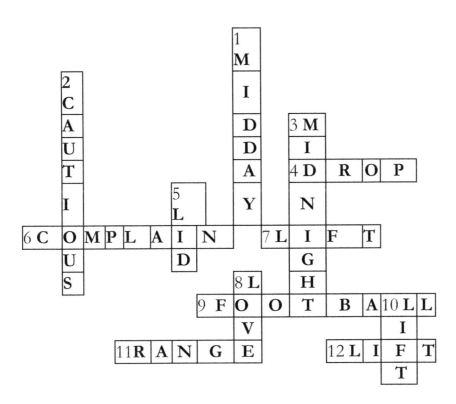

Episode Two

Some Grammar Revision Before We Start

This episode uses the **Past Perfect** as in *The Pasquatis had been to Britain before.*

The Past Perfect is a very important tense. It is used to show sequence (which event(s) came first) and the relationship between events (which event caused or resulted in another event).

Because of this, it is always used with another tense such as the Past Simple.

Remember, t is created by using HAD and the PAST PARTICIPLE OF THE VERB. E.g. To speak, spoke, **spoken**

As a diagram, it looks like this.

                X   X   NOW

I **had spoken** to my boss about this problem before. I **spoke** to him about

                                it again yesterday.

I **had written** 10 pages last week.   This week I **wrote** 3.

This can sometimes be reversed. E.g.

I **wrote** 3 pages this week but I **had written** 10 pages last week.

<u>One of the reasons that the Past Perfect is so important is that it clearly shows time and the link between events.</u>

For example:

The aircraft made an emergency landing at the airport. The engine failed.

This is unclear. It does not tell us clearly why the aircraft made an emergency landing. Was a passenger unwell? Where and when did the engine fail? Did the engine fail at the airport? But…

The aircraft **made** *an emergency landing at the airport because the engine* **had failed.**

This is clear.

Again: *The police* **shot** *and* **killed** *a robber. The robber* **shot** *at the police.*

This is again unclear because it is not 100% certain who started to shoot. But

*The police **shot** and **killed** a robber because the robber **had shot** at the police. [had shot at them* This is also possible.*]*

This is very clear and could be important in law.

The government built a new town. The country's population increased.

Again, this is unclear. Did the population increase before or after the government built the town?

*The government **built** a new town because the country's population **had increased.***

This is clear.

The Pasquatis Start to Plan

The Pasquatis had been to Britain before, but like many tourists they had spent a few days in London seeing what they thought were the main sights. Mr. Pasquati had little interest in history, but was happy to tell his friends that he had seen The Tower of London, the London Eye and Buckingham Palace. By comparison, Mr. MacDonald had a deep interest in history and had irritated Mr. Pasquati by pointing out the places the Pasquatis had missed and which he considered important.

The Tower of London as seen from the River Thames. The Norman invaders built the main building, the White Tower, soon after 1066. A main purpose was to control the Anglo-Saxon Londoners.

Mr. Pasquati's wife was happy to tag along (1) with her husband, but she insisted on going to the National Gallery because she loved art. She also insisted on going to Oxford Street with the intention to buy some new clothes, but found nothing within her budget that interested her. At the time both Pietro and Francesca were quite young and did what most young children do when dragged away from friends and home- they complained.

The family had also made day trips to Oxford and Cambridge, as most of their friends had done, but had not visited Edinburgh, the other popular destination. Pietro had enjoyed Cambridge. The weather was good that day, the sunniest day of the week, and his Dad had paid to take what they all thought was a strange boat out on the local river, the Cam. Pietro remembered the boat was called a punt and it was moved by pushing a pole into the bed (2) of the river and then pulling it out before the boat moved forward. Mr.

Pasquati had been too slow and Pietro could not stop laughing when his Dad fell into the river. Mr. Pasquati did not forgive him for the next week.

The MacDonalds had invited them to stay with them in their house for a fortnight near a town called Inverness. The Pasquatis easily found Inverness on *Google Earth* but were shocked to see how far north it was. It appeared to be miles from both London and Edinburgh and, somehow, they had imagined that Edinburgh was closer to London. It was a problem for Mr. Pasquati who had never driven far in Britain, and he was upset to see the distance his wife expected him to drive on the wrong side of the road.

The main road from London north on the eastern side of the country, the A1, went past towns and cities which were totally unknown to him. Francesca had developed an interest in history at school and was intrigued to discover that much of the A1 was based on the old Roman road called *Ermine Street* which ran from London to a city called Lincoln. She immediately decided it was worth a detour to see this. At this point Mr. Pasquati put his foot down (3) and decided that, because he had been volunteered to do all the driving by his wife, he was going to plan the journey. He actually liked planning and controlling the family's holiday. The next thing the family knew, they were booked on a flight to London leaving on August 2ⁿᵈ.

Italians might see similarities between punting and Venetian gondolas.

Language Notes

(1) **to tag along** To go with someone or a group, for company or to avoid problems, but perhaps without much interest.

(2) **bed** The river or sea bed is where the water meets soil or rock.

(3) *Mr. Pasquati* **put his foot down**. If someone puts their foot down it indicates that, for them, there is no further discussion or room for negotiation. *My Dad put his foot down when I told him that I wanted to stay out all night.*

Cultural Note

Ermine Street linked London with Lincoln and York. York was the capital of England for some time and Ermine Street has been in use for approximately 1,800 years.

It was called Ermine Street because all three cities had bishops or archbishops who wore ermine (a type of fur) as part of their religious dress.

Comprehension

1. *seeing what they thought were the main sights*

   Which of the following is both accurate in terms of language and the meaning of this extract?

   a) They saw a number of sites in London but perhaps not the most important.
   b) They actually saw the main sights in London
   c) They saw a number of sights in London but perhaps not the most important.
   d) They actually saw the main sites in London.

2. *Mr. MacDonald had irritated Mr. Pasquati by pointing out the places they had missed.*

   Which of the following is closest in meaning to…. *by pointing out the places they had missed.*

   a) The two men were travelling together and Mr. MacDonald showed Mr. Pasquati places to visit.
   b) Mr. MacDonald told Mr. Pasquati about the places he hadn't visited because of time.
   c) Mr. MacDonald told Mr. Pasquati about the places the family hadn't visited, but he thought were important.
   d) Mr. MacDonald pointed to places on the map which he thought it was important to visit.
   e) Mr. MacDonald told Mr. Pasquati about the places he should have visited.

3. [Mrs Pasquati] *also insisted on going to Oxford Street with the intention to buy some new clothes, but found nothing within her budget that interested her.*

   Which of these is correct according to the information in the passage?
   a) Mrs Pasquati could not afford to spend much money on clothes.
   b) Mrs Pasquati had decided how much she wanted to spend and the types of clothes she wanted to buy.
   c) Mrs Pasquati found Oxford Street clothes both boring and too expensive.
   d) Mrs Pasquati had a budget for her new clothes but they had to be the right type for her.

4. *At this point Mr. Pasquati put his foot down and decided that, because he had been volunteered to do all the driving by his wife, he was going to plan the journey.*

Which of the following are **NOT** mentioned as factors which made Mr. Pasquati decide to put his foot down?

Strange car	Distance	Unfamiliarity	Tiring
Side of the road	Arrival time	Weather	Distraction
Detours	Lincoln	Liked planning	

5. *he had been volunteered to do all the driving by his wife*

This means that:

a) He volunteered to drive some of the way.
b) Mrs. Pasquati allowed him to volunteer to do all the driving.
c) He volunteered to drive all the way.
d) Mrs. Pasquati told her husband that he had to do all the driving.

Some Practice of the Past Perfect

Which of these sentences is **grammatically correct and most precise?**

If there is new vocabulary here, make sure you learn it.

1. I left my friend at the bus stop, but turned back when I realised she left her purse in the car.
2. I had left my friend at the bus stop, but turned back when I realised she had left her purse in the car.
3. The waiter forgot to serve all the food we ordered, so I complained to the manager.
4. We had been to the restaurant before, and that day the waiter forgot to serve all the food we ordered so I complained to the manager.
5. We had been to the restaurant before, and that day the waiter had forgotten to serve all the food we had ordered so I had complained to the manager.
6. My friend missed his flight an accident blocked the road to the airport.
7. My friend missed his flight because there was an accident which blocked the road to the airport.
8. My friend missed his flight because there had been an accident which had blocked the road to the airport.
9. I dropped my boarding pass at the entrance to the terminal but someone found it and handed it to a police officer who contacted my carrier. I immediately ran back to get it.
10. I'd dropped my boarding pass at the entrance to the terminal but someone had found it and had handed it to a police officer who contacted my carrier. I immediately ran back to get it.

Crossword (There are some links to the story so far).

Crossword Clues

Across
7. The political capital of Italy.
10. Sea south of the Adriatic.
11. What you get with the right amount of sun
13. About the same.
14. The sun is highest in the sky.
15. Ancient buried city in Italy.

Down
1. The British think this Italian drink is too fast.
2. I'm not interested.
3. The sun can do this to you and you can with a cat or dog.
4. In the picture, she was not standing in the front but behind. People have one of these too.
5. The commercial capital of Italy.

6. We cannot live without this because it's exxxxxxxx.

8. To argue - perhaps not about something important.

9. The Pasquatis have at least one and Shakespeare said that Juliet stood on one.

12. University qualification. Mr Pasquati has one.

ANSWERS

1. *seeing what they thought were the main sights*

   b) is the correct answer.

   Sites has a different meaning. For example, the site of a battle (where the battle occurred) or a building site (where construction is taking place).

   This is different from seeing/visiting the *sights* which is used when seeing things such as in tourism.

   Note. It is possible for the two to be combined in the same sentence. For example: *One of the <u>sights</u> we saw in London was the Monument which marks the <u>site</u> where the Great Fire of London started in 1666.*

   The viewing tower of the Monument in London. It is now generally accepted that the fire accidentally started in a baker's shop, though a Frenchman was executed for starting it because of the anti-French hysteria at the time.

2. *Mr. MacDonald had irritated Mr. Pasquati by pointing out the places they had missed.*
   Which of the following is closest in meaning to…. *by pointing out the places they had missed?*

   c) **This is the correct answer.** *pointing out the places <u>they</u> had missed.*

   In this context, *they* refers to *the family.*

   by pointing out can be used to point at something or somebody, but it has wider meanings such as:

   My teacher pointed out that my work was full of mistakes. [pointed out here has the meaning of draw attention to/ show me my mistakes].

3. *My Dad wanted me to be home for ten, but when I argued with him my Mum pointed out that I was probably old enough to stay out a bit later.* [Here, the meaning is closer **to draw attention to a possible fact**].

4. *Mrs Pasquati] also insisted on going to Oxford Street with the intention to buy some new clothes, but found nothing within her budget that interested her.*

   e) is the answer. *nothing within her budget.* She had decided how much she wanted to spend **and** they had to interest her i.e. had to be the right type for her.

5. Which of the following are NOT mentioned as factors which made Mr. Pasquati decide to *put his foot down?*
   Strange car *Unfamiliarity* *Arrival time* *Weather* *Distraction*

6. *he had been volunteered to do all the driving by his wife*

   d) Mrs. Pasquati **told** her husband that he had to do all the driving.

Crossword Answers

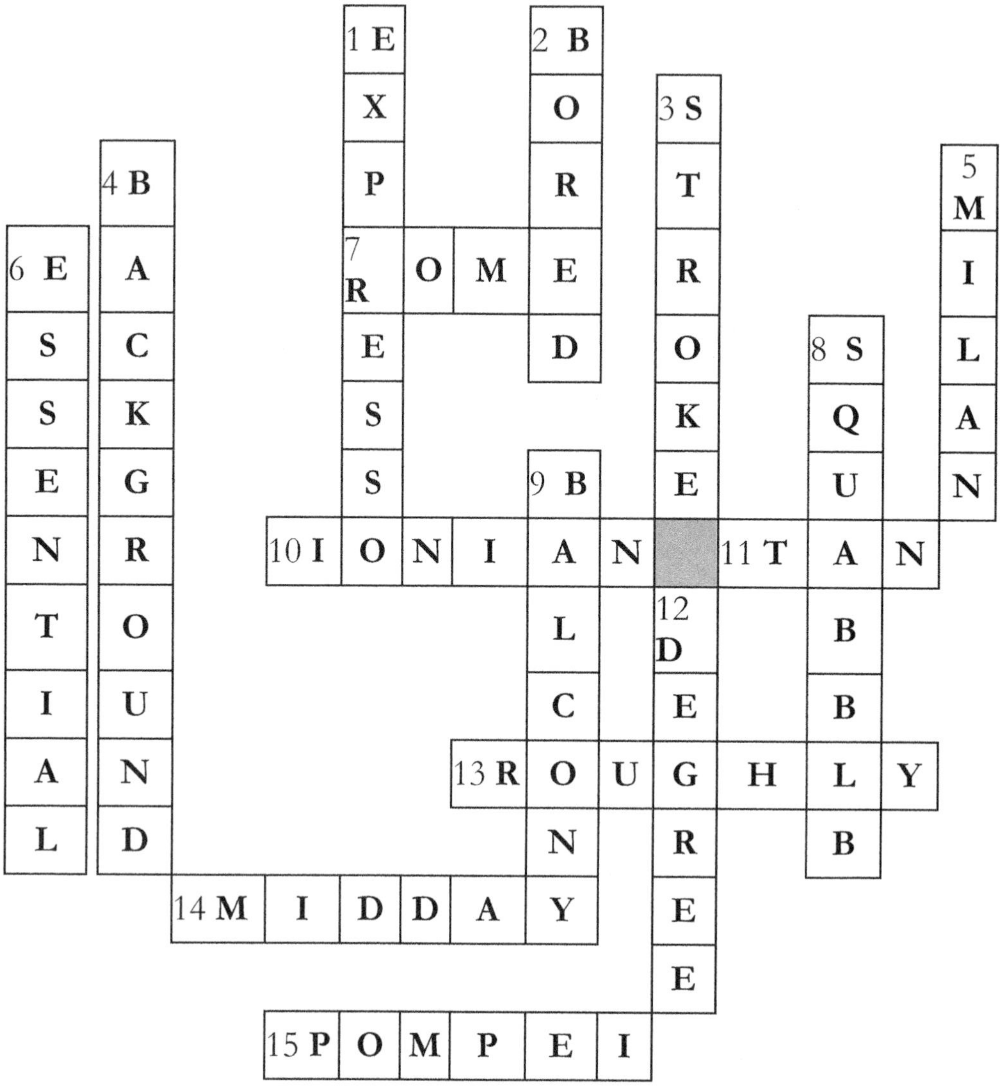
1 EXPRESS
2 BORED
3 STROKE
4 BACKGROUND
5 MILAN
6 ESSENTIAL
7 ROME
8 SQUABBLE
9 BALCONY
10 IONIAN
11 TAN
12 DEGREE
13 ROUGHLY
14 MIDDAY
15 POMPEI

Some Practice of the Past Perfect

Which of these sentences is **grammatically correct <u>and most precise</u>?**

If there is new vocabulary here, make sure you learn it.

1. I left my friend at the bus stop, but I turned back when I realised she left her purse in the car.
   This is incorrect. Two things had happened which caused the driver to turn back. A) The driver **had left** the friend at the bus stop and B) she **had left** her purse in the car.

2. I had left my friend at the bus stop, but turned back when I realised she had left her purse in the car.
   This is correct.

3. The waiter forgot to serve all the food we ordered, so I complained to the manager.
   This is incorrect. The waiter **had forgotten** to serve all the food, and this happened before the complaint *so I complained.*
   Irregular, common verb: Forget / Forgot/Forgotten

4. We had been to the restaurant before, and that day the waiter forgot to serve all the food we ordered so I complained to the manager.
   This is incorrect. Before is the key word and so events after should be in the past perfect. the waiter **had forgotten, so I had complained.**

5. We had been to the restaurant before, and that day the waiter had forgotten to serve all the food we had ordered so I had complained to the manager.
   This is the correct version.

6. My friend missed his flight an accident blocked the road to the airport.
   This is incorrect. The accident happened before the friend missed the flight.

7. My friend missed his flight because there had been an accident which had blocked the road to the airport.

8. **This is correct.** The cause of missing the flight was the accident **which had blocked** the road to the airport.

9. I dropped my boarding pass at the entrance to the terminal but someone found it and handed it to a police officer who contacted my carrier. I immediately ran back to get it.
   This is incorrect.

10. I'd dropped my boarding pass at the entrance to the terminal, but someone had found it and had handed it to a police officer who contacted my carrier. I immediately ran back to get it.

This is correct. The events which had started everything were because **I'd [I had] dropped** my boarding pass and then **someone had found it and had handed it to a police officer.**

The more recent events were: A) The *police officer contacted* the carrier and so B) *I immediately ran back to get it.*

Episode 3

A Bad Start to the Holiday

The family's (1) flight on August 2nd was at ten past eight from Bologna International and they needed to check in two hours beforehand. Normally, Mr. Pasquati would have suggested staying at a hotel near the airport the night before, but he had already arranged an important business meeting for the Friday evening of August 1st. This was the evening before their departure, but he was not prepared to cancel the meeting for fear of offending his clients.

There should have been no problem, because Mrs. Pasquati usually arranged all the packing, but that Friday Francesca suddenly announced that she wanted to go to a club with friends and HAD (2) to wear a particular dress which her mother had already packed in one of the suitcases. Her mother could not remember which suitcase, so much of Mrs. Pasquati's careful packing was undone as Francesca looked through the cases.

Mr. Pasquati finally arrived home towards eleven with mixed feelings about the meeting. He had been confident that his clients would sign the crucial contract that evening, and had taken them to a very expensive restaurant on that basis. But one of them suddenly started to try and renegotiate the contract so much that Mr. Pasquati saw his profit disappearing. The evening ended with the contract unsigned and Mr. Pasquati was much poorer after he had paid the bill. And (3) then Francesca failed to arrive home.

She'd (4) promised to be back before midnight, but it was after two when she finally turned up (5). Only then did Mr. Pasquati remember that his passport was in the safe at the office, over thirty minutes' drive in the wrong direction. The result was that they had to leave around five, drive to the office and then take the motorway north.

Everyone was in a bad mood when they got into the car that morning. Mrs. Pasquati was angry with her husband because of the extra journey, because he had come home late and with Francesca because she had been so thoughtless. Francesca was tired and, though she dared not admit this to her parents, had drunk too much and had a terrible hangover. Mr. Pasquati was angry with both himself and his clients. Only Pietro was left in a good mood. He had gone to bed early, slept well and was secretly enjoying his sister's discomfort. *That'll teach her to drink less*, he thought to himself. Usually he was the one who drank too much when he was out with his university mates (6) but was enjoying his sister's discomfort.

Pietro's good mood vanished as soon as they reached the slip road (7) onto the motorway. At that time on a Saturday the motorway was normally quite empty, but that morning every lane was full of slow-moving vehicles. When they turned on the radio there was a traffic announcement concerning a crash at the next junction, and Mrs. Pasquati totally lost her temper. *If your Dad hadn't left his passport at the office we would have joined two junctions further north,* she almost shouted, and looked anxiously at her watch.

We have time, Mr. Pasquati commented. He was trying to reduce the tension. At a quarter past seven they finally reached the airport and the family dashed to the check-in with their cases. They left Mr. Pasquati to park the car in the multi-storey and he ran into the airport holding only his passport. He found his family standing in front of one of the *Departures* boards.

Delayed an hour, Francesca announced.

Told you we should have booked with Ryanair, Pietro immediately said. He liked being right and had told his Dad to book with the budget airline rather than the national carrier.

At this point Mrs. Pasquati decided it was time to support her husband. *Well Pietro, I think your Dad did a great job getting us here despite that traffic. I know you've been earning quite a lot with your weekend job, so you can treat us all to some breakfast. We can relax for a while.*

Francesca struggled to stop herself from laughing as the grin disappeared from her brother's face.

Language Notes

(1) Remember the use of the possessive ` [The Anglo-Saxon genitive] which replaced *The flight of the family* many centuries ago. It is important to remember this when writing and speaking.

Note the difference between this and ` in (4) where it has a totally different function.

(2) **HAD** The use of capitals here is a quick, simple way to communicate. It is a little like shouting on the page. This technique is often used in plays but must not be used often in essays.

(3) **And.** There was a time when students were taught never to start a sentence with words such as *And* or *But.* But, English has become much more flexible in recent years and it is now acceptable.

But, if you are taking an exam, do what your teacher says!

(4) Remember that ` also symbolises the absence of letters in both <u>informal writing</u> and speech as well as the Anglo-Saxon genitive. Here, it represents *She had*

Can you remember the others?

I'd, You'd, She'd, He'd, We'd. They'd.

(5) **Turned up.** In this context arrived / came back home. To turn up implies an unplanned, unexpected or possibly unwanted event. It is often associated with arrival.

Examples: *We were sitting watching television when some old friends turned up. I hadn't heard from them for over three years.*

The police turned up soon after I rang them, but the thieves had already left.

My daughter turned up at the house on Saturday evening with a new boyfriend.

We had arranged to meet at the cinema but he turned up so late that we missed the start of the film.

(6) **Mates**. This is not necessarily the same as friends. Mates may not be as close. You can be *matey* with someone but not share your more personal feelings and thoughts. This is still a word most often used between males.

(7) **Slip road** the road which allows you to enter or leave the motorway.

Cultural Notes

A junction is where two or more roads meet. On motorways roads are joined by a slip road.

A lane. In British culture a lane is normally a narrower version of a road.

Historically lanes were in rural areas-is that a rabbit or a hare waiting for a lift?

However, when motorways developed the same word was used to describe the divisions in the road to separate traffic going in the same direction.

Most motorways in Britain have three lanes, a hard shoulder (where you can only stop in an emergency) and slip roads to leave or enter the motorway

A standard question would be *Which road are you taking to London?* The reply might be *We* or *I'm) are taking the M6 motorway.*

Streets almost always have houses, pavements for pedestrians and a road. An example is 10 Downing Street where the British Prime Minister lives.

Downing was a spy who worked for both sides (king and Parliament) during the English Civil Wars 1642-1651. Some historians believe he gave the land on which 10 Downing Street was built as a way of saving his life.

Roads are for cars, but many streets are also called roads. Sorry! This is Britain and things evolve! London Road (Rd.) is probably a few hundred years younger that London Street (St.) because many of the streets were built along the old straight (street in older English) Roman roads.

As a basic rule, remember that it is safe to walk along a street because it will have a pavement, but a road may not have a pavement (it is *unpaved*) so may be less safe.

Comprehension

1. Which of the choices below is correct? You need to consider this carefully in context.

The family needed to be at the airport by:

a) 07.50
b) 08.10
c) 06.10
d) 06.50

2. On which day of the month was their flight?

3. Mr. Pasquati was not prepared to cancel the meal *for fear of offending his clients.*

a) Because he was frightened of his clients.
b) Because he was a very polite man.
c) Because his business was bankrupt and these clients could help him.
d) Because his business had not been doing very well and these clients could provide work.

4. *Francesca suddenly announced that she wanted to go to a club with friends and* **HAD** *to wear a particular dress which her mother had already packed in one of the suitcases.*

HAD is used here to:

a) Show that Francesca had no other dress which was suitable for the party.
b) Had no other dresses which she thought were suitable for the party.
c) Illustrate that Francesca insisted that she had no other dress which was suitable for the party.
d) Illustrate that Francesca was arguing with her mother because Mrs. Pasquati was reluctant to open the suitcases she had already packed.

5. *Mr. Pasquati finally arrived home towards eleven with mixed feelings about the meeting.*

Which is correct?

a) Mr. Pasquati arrived home at eleven o'clock and was unsure if the business meeting had been a success.
b) Mr. Pasquati arrived home around eleven o'clock and was unhappy that he had spent money on a meal which had not resulted in a successful business meeting.
c) Mr. Pasquati arrived home at eleven o'clock and was unhappy that he had spent money on the meal.
d) Mr. Pasquati arrived home at eleven o'clock and was unhappy that he had spent money on a meal during which one of his clients had tried to change the contract.

6. When the Pasquatis joined the motorway, they were:

a) All upset for different reasons and late because of the trip to Mr. Pasquati's office to collect his passport from his desk.
b) All, except Pietro, upset for different reasons and late because of the extra time involved in going to Mr. Pasquati's office to collect his passport.
c) All, except Pietro, upset for different reasons and late because of the accident on the motorway and the time involved in going to Mr. Pasquati's office to collect his passport from his desk.
d) All, except Pietro, upset for different reasons and late because of the need for Mr. Pasquati to go to his office to collect his passport.
e) All, except Pietro, upset for different reasons and late because of the extra time involved in their going to Mr. Pasquati's office to collect his passport.

7. Which of the following most accurately describes Pietro?

a) He liked drinking with his school friends but enjoyed seeing his sister unwell.
b) He liked being right all the time and had given his Dad good advice about the flight.

c) He liked drinking with his school friends, enjoyed seeing his sister unwell and had a part-time job.

d) He enjoyed seeing his sister unwell, had a part-time job, but did not like spending his money.

A Crossword for You to Try

Crossword Clues

Across	Down
2. Oxford's wet crossing place	**1.** The person living at No. 10
3. Land meets sea	**5.** Being careful
4. Scotland's commercial capital	**6.** Part of a country
7. I'm interested but puzzled	**8.** To guide a vehicle, ship or aircraft
10. Cambridge and Oxford in the short form	**9.** Not the most direct route
13. Not interested	**11.** Typically red in London, but usually slow.
14. About the same	**12.** The industrial capital of Scotland
15. Not a good surprise	**16.** Cambridge's river
17. Done willingly	

ANSWERS

1. Which of the choices below is correct? You need to consider this carefully in context.

The family needed to be at the airport by:

c). 06.10 The family's flight on August 2ⁿᵈ was at **ten past eight** from Bologna International and they **needed to check in two hours beforehand**

2. On which day of the month was their flight? **Saturday.**

Mr. Pasquati *had already arranged an important business meeting for the F*riday **evening** *of August* 1ˢᵗ. *This was* **the evening before their departure…**

3. Mr. Pasquati was not prepared to cancel the meal for fear of offending his clients.

d) Because his business had not been doing very well and these clients could provide work.

It was a *crucial contract*

But one of them suddenly started to try and renegotiate the contract so much that Mr. Pasquati saw his profit disappearing.

4. *Francesca suddenly announced that she wanted to go to a club with friends and* **HAD** *to wear a particular dress which her mother had already packed in one of the suitcases.*

HAD *is used here to:*

e) Illustrate that Francesca was arguing with her mother because Mrs. Pasquati was reluctant to open the suitcases she had already packed.

Her mother could not remember which suitcase, so much of Mrs. Pasquati's careful packing was undone as Francesca looked through the cases.

5. Mr. Pasquati finally arrived home towards eleven with mixed feelings about the meeting.

f) Mr. Pasquati arrived home at eleven o'clock and was unhappy that he had spent money on a meal during which one of his clients had tried to change the contract.

There is no evidence that the meal had been a complete failure as in b). *Mr. Pasquati arrived home around eleven o'clock and was unhappy that he had spent money on a meal which* **had not resulted in a successful business meeting.**

It is not certain that the attempt to change the contract will result in failure –perhaps only a delay.

6. When the Pasquatis joined the motorway, they were:

This required some careful reading.

a) All upset for different reasons and late because of the trip to Mr. Pasquati's office to collect his passport from his desk. **Wrong. The passport was in the safe.**
b) All, except Pietro, upset for different reasons and late because of the extra time involved in going to Mr. Pasquati's office to collect his passport. **Wrong. No mention of the family going to the office.**
c) All, except Pietro, upset for different reasons and late because of the accident on the motorway and the time involved in going to Mr. Pasquati's office to collect his passport from his desk. **Wrong. The passport was in the safe. The accident on the motorways was unknown at the time.**
d) All, except Pietro, upset for different reasons and late because of the need for Mr. Pasquati to go to his office to collect his passport. **Wrong. Mr. Pasquati did not go alone.**
e) All, except Pietro, upset for different reasons and late because of the extra time involved in **their going** to Mr. Pasquati's office to collect his passport. **Correct. All the family travelled to the office.**

7. Which of the following most accurately describes Pietro?

d) *He enjoyed seeing his sister unwell, had a part-time job, but did not like spending his money.*

Usually he was the one who drank too much when he was out with his university mates **but was enjoying his sister's discomfort.**

At this point Mrs. Pasquati decided it was time to support her husband. Well Pietro, I think your Dad did a great job getting us here despite that traffic. I know **you've been earning quite a lot with your weekend job,** *so* **you can treat us all to some breakfast.** *We can chill out for a while.*

*Francesca struggled to stop herself from laughing as **the grin disappeared** from her brother's face.*

Crossword Answers

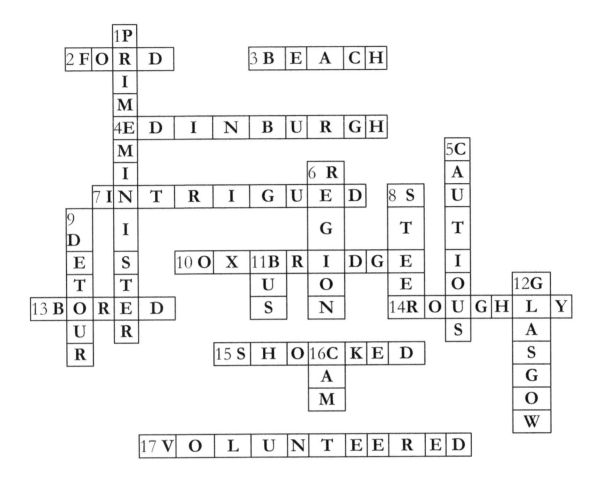

Episode 4

Bad News at the Airport

The family had cleared security and passport control and were exploring what the café in the Departures Lounge had to offer. *It's really kind of you to treat us all to breakfast Pietro,* Francesca said, smiling sweetly and adding a third pastry to her plate. She usually only ate one pastry and drank an expresso for breakfast, but this morning she was determined to irritate her brother by spending as much of his money as possible.

Her Dad seemed to have the same idea and had already piled a plate full of pastries which he put alongside a bowl of muesli on his tray. Only Mrs. Pasquati seemed to be eating as normal and was about to pay for the entire family when her husband put his hand on hers. As usual, she was about to take her purse from her handbag. *He needs to learn,* Mr. Pasquati whispered to Lucia, his wife, and she reluctantly closed the zip on her bag.

Pietro was also reluctant to pay, but the girl at the till was about his age, and very attractive, so he did not wish to appear mean. He looked hopefully at both his parents before realising that he actually had to pay this time and finally took his small rucksack from his back and dug into it to find his wallet. He stood at the check-out as the cashier added the items to the till and was relieved to find that the total bill of 38 euros was less than he had feared, but still nearly the amount that the local gardener usually paid him on a daily basis for helping at the weekend. He and his Dad carried the two trays to a corner seat and sat down, keen to at least drink some coffee.

Forgot something?

Pietro looked up and found a middle-aged man standing over him and holding his rucksack.

I think this is yours. You'll miss it later, and he handed the bag to Pietro. Lucia tended to be over-cautious in most things and, as the man passed the bag, he glanced at the label she had attached to the bag. It was totally unnecessary as Pietro's computer was inside and he never-normally- let it out of his sight. *Have you decided not to go?* The man asked, clearly puzzled.

What do you mean? Pietro asked. *Our flight to Stansted has been delayed.*

But your baggage label is for Gatwick and the gate is closed for that, the man replied, glancing up at one of the screens.

Mr. Pasquati was normally a calm, gentle man and his family had never before seen him do what he did in the next few seconds. Jumping to his feet, and almost knocking over the table, he almost choked as his coffee returned to its cup. Then, there was a barely controlled scream as he checked his tickets twice and looked at the Departures screen once, twice and a final third time before he shouted to the family *Quickly! Run! We may make it!*

Five minutes later they arrived at the boarding gate. There was only one person who was checking through the boarding passes. *Family Pasquatis?* she enquired. *You've missed your flight you know. Didn't you hear the final call? Your luggage has been taken off the flight. You can collect it from one of the luggage belts on your way out.*

But surely, it's not too late! Lucia asked between tears.

It was the traffic. Wasn't it? The attendant asked. The question was intended to be helpful. *Tell my colleague on the front desk. I'm sorry you will have to go through passport control again. My colleague may be able to get you seats on the next flight. Mr. Pasquati is a regular, so we'll do what we can to help.*

When is the next available flight? Francesca asked, fearing the worst.

I'm afraid the 15.00 is full, but there are seats on the 18.00. So, you can get to London for the evening.

Ah. Not where we are going, Pietro snapped. (1)

Apologies for my son, he needs to learn some manners, Mr. Pasquati interrupted, seeing the change on the attendant's face and the possibility of their evening flight disappearing. *We are actually going to Scotland.*

From Gatwick? The long-way round the flight attendant queried. *What was wrong with Stansted? Much further north.*

I like flying with you, Mr. Pasquati immediately replied, trying to save their evening seats. *You are such a good company.*

The woman smiled. *I'll do what I can to arrange a cost-free transfer. I'm here all day so may see you later. Don't forget to see my colleagues - and do have a good day.*

The four stood silently for a few seconds before Pietro announced: *So, we can go home for a few hours. I have an online game I want to finish with Michele.*

But I want to go and look at the shops, Francesca said, using a special *little girl's voice* which she used when she wanted to influence her father. *Bologna has such wonderful shops and this place in Scotland is so.........so isolated.*

This time she was unsuccessful. *Don't think for a second that I'm driving us back home and then coming back here in a few hours,* Mr. Pasquati said firmly. *Your Mum said a few weeks ago that she wanted to see an exhibition at one of the galleries in Bologna. I'm happy to finish my breakfast in town and then have a look around. I have not been here for years as a tourist. We need to get our cases, put them back in the car and then get the shuttle bus into town. I've had enough of driving for a day.*

Bus? Pietro queried. *Can't you drive us in?*

It's the bus or you can walk, Mr. Pasquati replied. He took Lucia hand and walked off.

Language Notes

1. **Snapped** is used here to communicate a rude, short comment. It is often used to communicate anger, difficulty and stress.

Some examples. *She was so angry when she discovered that her husband had spent all their money on a new television that **she snapped** and threw a bottle through its screen.*

*A combination of heat and humidity can cause many people **to snap** and become very violent.*

*He had been under a lot of pressure at work for several months. One Friday afternoon **he finally snapped**, walked out of the office, and was never seen again.*

You are late again! **He snapped**. *And now we have missed the start of the show.*

Comprehension

1. *It's really kind of you to treat us all to breakfast Pietro Francesca said, smiling sweetly and adding a third pastry to her plate.*

In the context of the paragraph, which of the following most accurately reflects this extract:

a) Francesca is thanking her brother for being so generous.
b) Francesca is being sarcastic and using the opportunity to upset her brother because of something he did earlier.
c) Francesca is thanking her brother for being so generous and is using the opportunity to have a good breakfast.
d) Francesca is being sarcastic and using the opportunity to upset her brother because of the nature of their relationship.

2. *Pietro was also reluctant – to pay. He looked hopefully at both his parents before realising that he actually had to pay this time.*

In the context of the paragraph, which of the following most accurately reflects this extract:

a) Pietro's Mum often asked him to pay but then paid herself.
b) Pietro had seen his Mum open her handbag to take out her purse.
c) Pietro's parents often asked him to pay but then paid themselves.
d) Pietro wanted to save his money for the holiday and hoped that his parents would pay this time.

3. *…the total bill of 38 euros was less than he had feared, but still nearly the amount that the local gardener usually paid him on a daily basis for helping at the weekend.*

Pietro had:

a) Expected the bill to be more than 38 euros which was his usual weekend earnings.
b) Been worried that he would not have enough money to pay the bill.
c) Had worked with a gardener at the weekend and had earned 38 euros which he did not want to spend.
d) Worked with a gardener at the weekends and did not want to spend his weekend earnings on the family's breakfast.

4. *It was totally unnecessary as Pietro's computer was inside and he never - normally - let it out of his sight.*

Normally is used here because:

a) Pietro had paid for breakfast, which was unusual for him, and he had done something unusual because he had forgotten his rucksack at the till.
b) Pietro had been upset by the events of the morning and he had done something unusual because he had forgotten his rucksack.
c) Pietro had perhaps been distracted by the girl working in the café and that, combined with the cost of paying, had distracted him enough to forget his rucksack.
d) He planned to go back for his rucksack after he and his father had taken the trays to the table, but had forgotten to do so.

5. Use the information **from all the story** to find examples of Pietro and Francesca being selfish. You need to look at evidence from all the units.

A Gap Filling Exercise:

At the airport

The words listed below relate to airports and travel. You need to insert them in the correct gaps in this section. If you have not travelled by air before, ask your parents of friends to help you.

shuttle	radar	E-tickets	runways	terminal	security
embark	scheduled	storey	luggage	scan	scanned
Lounge	hold	screens	stow	belt	

The first thing I saw when we approached the airport was the tall control tower with a _____ system on top of it used to monitor the arrival and departure of aircraft. Then, when we got closer, I saw there was a long, tall fence. On the far side of the fence a few aircraft were parked on one of the _____.

Mum was driving, and she dropped us and our _____ at the _____ before she drove the car into the multi-_____ car park. As soon as she joined us we checked our flight on one of the Departures _____ and then went to the check-in desk. Dad had already checked in on line, so it took only a few seconds to _____ our E-tickets and pass our luggage for the attendant to put on the _____ which carried it away. My parents explained that they put these, big cases in the _____ of the aircraft but that we could _____ our small bags above our seats on the aircraft.

Then we had to scan our _____ again as we passed through _____ and then our hand luggage was put on a different belt and it went through a type of tunnel. It was my first flight but my sister had flown before and she explained that the security personnel _____ the bags to make sure there was nothing illegal or dangerous in them. After we had cleared security we walked through a long corridor lined with duty free shops which Mum told me were supposed to offer things at lower prices than normal shops. We stopped to have something to eat and drink before we went to the Departure _____ where we sat and I listened to some of my music with my sister.

It was a long time before the announcement came for us to _____ and we had to show our tickets and passports again before we got on a _____ bus which took us across the runway to our waiting aircraft. The aircraft had landed late, so we left about twenty minutes after our _____ departure time.

ANSWERS

1. *It's really kind of you to treat us all to breakfast Pietro Francesca said, smiling sweetly and adding a third pastry to her plate.*

   d) is the correct answer. Francesca is being sarcastic using the opportunity to upset her brother because of the nature of their relationship.

2. *Pietro was also reluctant – to pay. He looked hopefully at both his parents before realising that he actually had to pay this time.*

   c) is the correct answer. Pietro's parents often asked him to pay but then paid themselves.

3. *…the total bill of 38 euros was less than he had feared, but still nearly the amount that the local gardener usually paid him on a daily basis for helping at the weekend.*

   Pietro had: a) Expected the bill to be more than 38 euros which was his usual weekend earnings.

4. *It was totally unnecessary as Pietro's computer was inside and he never -**normally** - let it out of his sight.* **Normally** is used here because

   a) Pietro had paid for breakfast, which was unusual for him, and he had done something unusual because he had forgotten his rucksack at the till.

5. **Being selfish:**

   Pietro
   - Enjoyed seeing his sister suffer.
   - Showed no sympathy when his dad was under pressure (e.g. criticised his choice of flight).
   - Was reluctant to pay for breakfast.
   - Wanted to go back home so that he could play his game.
   - Didn't want to take the bus into Bologna –he wanted his Dad to drive them in.
   - Perhaps snapping at the lady at the gate? This could be seen as being selfish – she was only doing her job and was trying to be helpful

   Francesca
   - **Had** to have one dress even though her Mum had packed the cases.
   - Came home late and worried her parents.
   - Got drunk the night before their departure- she was not in a good state to travel the following day.
   - Enjoyed seeing Pietro suffer when he spent his money.
   - Took more food than usual for breakfast to make Pietro spend more money.

- Immediately wanted to go shopping in Bologna without thinking of others.

A Gap Filling Exercise:

At the airport

The first thing I saw when we approached the airport was the tall control tower   with a **radar** system on top of it used to monitor the arrival and departure of aircraft. Then, when we got closer, I saw there was a long, tall fence. On the far side of the fence a few aircraft were parked on one of the **runways.**

Mum was driving, and she dropped us and our **luggage** at the **terminal** before she drove the car into the multi-**storey** car park. As soon as she joined us we checked our flight on one of the Departures **screens** and then went to the check-in desk. Dad had already checked in on line, so it took only a few seconds to **scan** our E-tickets and pass our luggage for the attendant to put on the **belt** which carried it away. My parents explained that they put these, big cases in the **hold** of the aircraft but that we could **stow** our small bags above our seats on the plane.

Then we had to scan our **E-tickets** again as we passed through **security** and then our hand luggage was put on a different belt and it went through a type of tunnel. It was my first flight but my sister had flown before and she explained that the security personnel **scanned** the bags to make sure there was nothing illegal or dangerous in them. After we had cleared security we walked through a long corridor lined with duty free shops which Mum told me were supposed to offer things at lower prices than normal shops. We stopped to have something to eat and drink before we went to the Departure **Lounge** where we sat and I listened to some of my music with my sister.

It was a long time before the announcement came for us to **embark** and we had to show our tickets and passports again before we got on a **shuttle** bus which took us across the runway to our waiting aircraft. The aircraft had landed late, so we left about twenty minutes after our **scheduled** departure time.

Episode Five

A Confusing Day

A Reminder

The Pasquatis had met (1) the McDonalds while on holiday in Italy and they had soon become (1) good friends. The start of the journey was problematic (2). Mr Pasquati had left (1) his passport in his office and had also made (1) the mistake of booking a flight to the wrong London airport. As a result, we left (3) the family in Bologna where they were waiting (4) for an evening flight to London.

....

Some Grammar Points

1. Think carefully about the grammar from the first few lines above and notice the use of the past perfect.

2. Something is *problematic* when it creates or contains problems or difficulties. Some example:

Removing that tooth will be quite **problematic** *because of the way it has grown,* said the dentist. *You should have come to see me earlier.*

Our children have a **problematic** *relationship. For some reason they really dislike each other, so they are always fighting.*

I'm happy to lend you the money, but it's all invested and it will be **problematic** *to get it before the end of the month.*

3. **We left** This contains two elements. *We* is used here as part of a narrative style which is designed to encourage the reader to feel involved in the story. It is a very traditional style used at the start of some stories or to involve the reader in the written work.

Notice that **We left** is past simple. Why? Because it is a finished event in the past.

4. *they were waiting* This is using the **Past Continuous** to describe an **unfinished** action/event in the past or an action in the past which was interrupted. We shall look at this in more detail later.

A Short Grammar Test

Complete the gaps in these following.

In some cases the infinitive of the verb is provided.

1. I … already left the party when I realised that my mobile was still at my friend's house.
2. I …. driving to university when I ….. [to see] my friend Susan. She … standing at the bus stop waiting for a bus.
3. My car suddenly stopped because I … forgotten to fill the tank with fuel.
4. My parents were very angry when I arrived home late. I …. written a note for them and … left it on the table in the hall but they didn't see it. When I arrived home my Dad ….. standing at the front door.
5. My dentist said that I needed some work on my teeth. She thought that I …. eaten too many sweets.
6. I went to America for a holiday last year. The year before I ….. been to Sweden. It was the first time I had been away on my own and when I …… [to come] back after two weeks my parents ……. waiting for me at the airport.
7. I am studying very hard because I want to go to university next year. My sister …… [to pass] all her exams last year and now she is ……… [to study] medicine at university.

ANSWERS TO QUESTIONS

A Short Grammar Exercise I

1. I had already left the party when I realised that my mobile was still at my friend's house.

2. I was driving to university when I saw my friend Susan. She was standing at the bus stop waiting for a bus.

3. My car suddenly stopped because I had forgotten to fill the tank with fuel.

4. My parents were very angry when I arrived home late. I had written a note for them and had left it on the table in the hall but they didn't see it. When I arrived home my Dad was standing at the front door.

5. My dentist said that I needed some work on my teeth. She thought that I had eaten too many sweets.

6. I went to America for a holiday last year. The year before I had been to Sweden. It was the first time I had been away on my own and when I came back after two weeks my parents were waiting for me at the airport.

7. I am studying very hard because I want to go to university next year. My sister passed all her exams last year and now she is studying medicine at university.

The section below is from an earlier part of the story. Again, note where the Past Perfect tense is used (*past event followed by past event*). The past simple is mainly used after the past perfect in such sentences.

Bad News at the Airport

There are some new questions at the end of this section.

The family had cleared (1) security and passport control and were exploring what the café in the Departures Lounge had to offer. *It's really kind of you to treat us all to breakfast Pietro* Francesca said, smiling sweetly and adding a third pastry to her plate. She usually only ate one pastry and drank an expresso for breakfast, but this morning she was determined to irritate her brother by spending as much of his money as possible.

Her Dad seemed to have the same idea and had already piled a plate full of pastries which he put alongside a bowl of muesli on his tray. Only Mrs Pasquati seemed to be eating her normal breakfast, and she was about to pay for the entire family when her husband put his hand on hers. As usual, she was about to take her purse from her handbag. *He needs to learn* Mr Pasquati whispered to Lucia, his wife, and she reluctantly closed the zip on her bag.

Pietro was also reluctant to pay, but the girl at the till was about his age, and very attractive, so he did not wish to appear mean. He looked hopefully at both his parents before he realised that he actually had to pay this time and finally took his small rucksack from his back and dug into it to find his wallet. He stood at the check-out as the cashier added the items to the till and was relieved to find that the total bill of 38 euros was less than he had feared, but still nearly the amount that the local gardener usually paid him on a daily basis for helping at the weekend. He and his Dad carried the two trays to a corner seat and sat down, keen to at least drink some coffee.

Forgot something? Pietro looked up and found a middle-aged man standing over him and holding his rucksack. *I think this is yours. You'll miss it later* and he handed the bag to Pietro. Lucia tended to be over-cautious in most things and, as the man passed the bag, he glanced at the label she had attached to the bag. It was totally unnecessary as Pietro's computer was inside and he never-normally-let it out of his sight.

Have you decided not to go? The man asked, clearly puzzled.

What do you mean? Pietro asked. *Our flight to Stansted has been delayed.*

But your baggage label is for Gatwick and the gate is closed for that, the man replied, glancing up at one of the screens.

Mr Pasquati was normally a calm, gentle man and his family had never before seen him do what he did in the next few seconds. Jumping to his feet, and almost knocking over the table, he nearly choked as his coffee returned to its cup. Then, there was a barely controlled scream as he checked his tickets twice and looked at the Departures screen once, twice and a final third time before he shouted to the family *Quickly! Run! We may make it!*

Five minutes later they arrived at the boarding gate. There was only one person who was checking through the boarding passes. *Family Pasquati?* She enquired without looking up. *You've missed your flight you know. Didn't you hear the final call? Your luggage has been taken off the flight. You can collect it from one of the luggage belts on your way out.*

But surely, it's not too late! Lucia asked between tears.

The attendant looked up and immediately recognised Mr Pasquati. *It was the traffic. Wasn't it?* she asked. The question was intended to be helpful. *Tell my colleague on the front desk. I'm sorry you will have to go through passport control again. My colleague may be able to get you seats on the next flight. Mr Pasquati is a regular, so we'll do what we can to help.*

When is the next available flight? Francesca asked, fearing the worst.

I'm afraid the 15.00 is full, but there are seats on the 18.00. So, you can get to London for the evening.

Ah. Not where we are going, Pietro snapped.

Apologies for my son, he needs to learn some manners Mr Pasquati interrupted, seeing the change on the attendant's face and the possibility of their evening flight disappearing. *We are actually going to Scotland.*

From Gatwick? the flight attendant queried. *That's the long-way round! What was wrong with Stansted Airport? That is much further north.*

I like flying with you, Mr Pasquati immediately replied, trying to save their evening seats. *You are such a good company.*

The woman smiled. *I'll do what I can to arrange a cost-free transfer. I'm here all day so I may see you later. Don't forget to see my colleagues - and do have a good day.*

The four stood silently for a few seconds before Pietro announced: *So, we can go home for a few hours. I have an online game I want to finish with Michele.*

But I want to go and look at the shops, Francesca said, using a special *little girl's voice* which she used when she wanted to influence her father. *Bologna has such wonderful shops and this place in Scotland is so………isolated.*

This time she was unsuccessful. *Don't think for a second that I'm driving us back home and then coming back here in a few hours,* Mr Pasquati said firmly. *Your Mum said a few weeks ago that she wanted to see an exhibition at the gallery in Bologna and I'm happy to finish my breakfast in town and then have a look around. I have not been here for years as a tourist. We need to get our cases, put them back in the car and then get the shuttle bus into town. I have had enough of driving for a day.*

Bus? Pietro queried. *Can't you drive us in?*

Take the bus or you can walk, Mr Pasquati replied. He took Lucia's hand and walked off.

....

Some Vocabulary Explained

1. **to clear security** has the meaning of successfully passing through security.

To clear [sometimes clear up] has a general meaning of doing something / something happening / resolving a problem. Usually, there is a consequence for an event which follows.

Some useful examples:

The road was **clear** so we arrived home early.

The fog **cleared** so our flight was able to take-off on time.

We have guests coming, so please **clear** your stuff off the table so that I can set it.

You have upset your Mum. I don't know what the problem is, but she is very sad. Can you **clear up** the problem before you go out?

Is this explanation **clear**? If not, I can try to explain in a different way.

The fire service **cleared** the road from the trees which had fallen during the storm.

....

So, what can we learn about this family?

The clues are not only in the words, but in the actions. It is important to look for these small clues as they may help you to understand languages even if you don't know all the vocabulary.

Some examples:

It's really kind of you to treat us all to breakfast Pietro, Francesca said, smiling sweetly and adding a third pastry to her plate. She usually only ate one pastry and drank an expresso for breakfast, but this morning she was determined to irritate her brother by spending as much of his money as possible.

Notice that Francesca is *determined to spend as much money as possible* in order to irritate her brother, Pietro. This indicates some tension between the two.

Pietro was also reluctant to pay, but the girl at the till was about his age, and very attractive, so he did not wish to appear mean. So Pietro is…..how old? The cashier [the person who works at the till] is old enough to be working and Pietro is at university.

He (Pietro) stood at the check-out as the cashier added the items to the till and was relieved to find that the total bill of 38 euros was less than he had feared, but still nearly the amount that the local gardener usually paid him on a daily basis for helping at the weekend. So Pietro is not totally lazy.

Ah. Not where we are going, Pietro snapped.

Apologies for my son, he needs to learn some manners Mr Pasquati interrupted, seeing the change on the attendant's face and the possibility of their evening flight disappearing. *We are actually going to Scotland.* But Pietro is not diplomatic, and has a temper. He snaps [talks impolitely] at the lady who is trying to help the family.

Take the bus or you can walk Mr Pasquati replied. He took Lucia's hand and walked off. Lucia is Mr Pasquati's wife. He took her hand… to show solidarity? They walked off to ….? To end any possible discussion / argument?

…………………………

Grammar

The **past simple** *usually* describes a finished event in the past.

Finished Past Event   **Now**

      X

I went to Paris last year.

You can see that the **Past Event** and **Now** are not connected.

If you want to connect them, you need to add additional information.

So, *I went to Paris last year and <u>had a good time</u>* [additional information.]

We saw earlier that the **Past Perfect talks about an event which had happened before the Past Simple.**

I went to Paris last year and had a good time. I **had visited** *Paris the year before and I* **had experienced** *a very bad time.*

Can you see the shift from the Past Simple to the Past Perfect?

Sometimes <u>we need to describe a continuing event, or events, using the Past Continuous and this happens at the same time as another, finished event.</u> For example:

I was visiting *Paris last year when* **I met** *an old friend.*

I was visiting *[……* a continuing event in the past] *…… Paris last year when* **I met**

[**X** finished past event] *an old friend.*

The dots above …. represent a continuing event / activity in the past while the **X** represents a finished past event.

Further information can be provided by the past simple.

I was visiting *Paris last when* **I met** *an old friend. That evening* **we went** *for a drink.*

……………………………………..**X**…………………………………..**X**…………

Why does the dotted line continue? It continues because the person was still visiting Paris.

<u>Let us look at one part of the story and see how we can use these tenses.</u>

Pietro was also reluctant to pay, but the girl at the till was about his age, and very attractive, so he did not wish to appear mean. He looked hopefully at both his parents before he realised that he actually had to pay this time and finally took his small rucksack from his back and dug into it to find his wallet.

We can quickly make these questions using different tenses.

1. Was Pietro happy / reluctant to pay? [Past Simple]

No, he **was** not happy to pay.

 2. Where was the girl working? [Past Continuous]

The girl **was working** at the till.

3. What had Pietro done before he realised that he actually had to pay? [Past Perfect followed by Past Simple].

He **had looked** hopefully at both his parents before he **realised** that he had to pay.

4. Where had Pietro's rucksack been before he dug into it? [Past Perfect followed by Past Simple]

Pietro's rucksack **had been** on his back.

5. Where had Pietro's wallet been? [Past Perfect followed by Past Simple because we know that he dug into his rucksack.]

Pietro's wallet **had been** in his rucksack before he **dug** into his rucksack.

And a question for you from the text:

Where did this happen? [Past Simple. Finished action with no connection made].

It **happened** in the café at the airport.

These grammar issues are important, so look for them later in the story.

Comprehension and Vocabulary

1. What was similar in the behaviour of Francesca and her father in the café at the airport?

2. Where did Mrs Pasquati keep her money?

3. How much had Pietro expected the bill in the airport café to be?

4. Describe the middle-aged man who spoke to Pietro in the café.

5. Why was Mr Pasquati suddenly very upset?

6. Why did the attendant at the boarding gate mention the delay caused by traffic?

7. What advantages did Francesca see in their delayed flight?

A Short Grammar Test

The sentences below contain a mixture of past simple, past perfect and past continuous tenses. Which sentences are correct? Why?

Don't worry if you make some mistakes; we shall look at these tenses regularly.

1. I was waiting for a bus, which was 10 minutes late, when my friend arrived. She had been on a flight from Berlin.

2. I was waiting for a bus, which was 10 minutes late, when my friend arrived. She left Berlin a few minutes after mine.

3. I was waiting for a bus, which was 10 minutes late, when my friend arrived. She had left Berlin a few minutes after my flight had departed.

4. My friend flew from Berlin a few minutes after I had left. I met her at the bus stop after I had waited there for a bus for over 10 minutes.

5. I waited for a bus, which was 10 minutes late, when my friend arrived. She left Berlin a few minutes after my flight had left.

6. My friend flew from Berlin a few minutes after I left. I met her at the bus stop after I was standing there for 10 minutes.

Answers

1. Both Francesca and her father were eating more than usual for their breakfast. It seems that they wanted their breakfasts to cost a lot because Pietro was paying.

2. Mrs Pasquati had her money in her purse in her handbag. [Traditionally, a purse was associated with females and a wallet with males.]

3. He had expected that it would be more than 38 euros. *[(He) was relieved to find that the total bill of 38 euros was less than he had feared…]*

4. We can say two things about this man apart from the fact that he is middle-aged. The first thing we can say is that he is honest; he could have walked away with Pietro's bag and this could have contained valuable objects such as phones and computers. It actually contained Pietro's computer.

The second thing we can say is that he is observant. He **had noticed** that the luggage tag on Pietro's bag was for Gatwick and that the boarding gate for that flight **had already closed**. [Notice the two past perfects here. These events **had happened** before the man spoke to Pietro].

5. Mr Pasquati was upset because he had realised that he had made a mistake with the family's flight.

[In spoken English or informal writing it would be: *Mr Pasquati was upset because* **he'd** *realised that* **he'd** *made a mistake with the family's flight*].

6. The attendant was trying to be helpful and perhaps avoid charging the family for new tickets.

It's probably better to blame the traffic than to admit to being incompetent, which the family was. Mr Pasquati also mentioned that he flew regularly with this company (*I like flying with you* Mr Pasquati immediately replied, trying to save their evening seats. *You are such a good customer.*) The attendant recognised this regular customer because she later complimented him as *'a gentleman'*.

6. Francesca wanted to explore the shops in Bologna. She also considered their destination in Scotland *so………isolated,* so it may have been her last chance to shop before going away.

Answers to a Short Grammar Test

1. I was waiting for a bus, which was 10 minutes late, when my friend arrived. She had been on a flight from Berlin.

<u>This is grammatically correct.</u> This uses the past continuous to start the sentence. This is correct because the person *was waiting* for a bus when the friend arrived [past simple]. **Before the friend arrived at the bus stop** she **had been** on a flight from Berlin

2. I was waiting for a bus, which was 10 minutes late, when my friend arrived. She left Berlin a few minutes after my flight.

<u>Grammatically, this is not a correct use of tenses.</u> She had left Berlin after the first flight so *had left Berlin* is more precise. **However,** in modern English this is a commonly used structure in everyday speaking and writing. The misuse **in this situation** is not important. <u>It could be important in another situation and, especially in an examination, you should use the correct forms.</u>

3. I was waiting for a bus, which was 10 minutes late, when my friend arrived. She had left Berlin a few minutes after my flight had departed.

<u>This is grammatically correct.</u> Remember that in spoken English, reported speech and informal writing the **she had** would be **she'd.**

4. My friend flew from Berlin a few minutes after I had left. I met her at the bus stop after I had waited there for a bus for over 10 minutes.

<u>This is grammatically correct.</u> Remember that in spoken English, reported speech and informal writing the **I had** would be **I'd.**

5. I waited for a bus, which was 10 minutes late, when my friend arrived. She left Berlin a few minutes after my flight had left.

This is incorrect. **I waited for a bus** is past simple and implies a finished action. But the action was not finished. The friend arrived, and we know about her flight, but the two were still waiting for the bus.

6. My friend flew from Berlin a few minutes after I left. I met her at the bus stop after I was standing there for 10 minutes.

This is incorrect. The clue is in the word **after.** The friend **arrived** [past simple] **after I had been standing** there for 10 minutes. [This is Past Perfect Continuous. If you are unsure of this, don't worry because we shall look at it regularly].

A QUICK REMINDER

IT IS VERY EASY to forget the **S on the third person singular** and this quickly reduces the quality of your English. This is not because people will not understand you, but it is seen as an (irritating?) mistake.

Zoe like**s** ice cream.

Peter read**s** a book every week.

Harriett ride**s** her horse every weekend.

Lucy drive**s** a Fiat.

And then there is the question.

Do Zoe like ice cream? sounds very poor.

*Doe**s** Zoe like ice?* creates a clear idea that you know your English well.

Note that the **s** on the verb disappears because you are using the infinitive.

So *Does Lucy drive a Fiat?* and **NOT** *Does Lucy drives_a Fiat?*

Episode Six

The Journey Continues

The family needed to return to the airport at 16.00 to clear security. Francesca insisted on saying *At 4 o'clock in the afternoon* once she had discovered that the British seemed to dislike the 24 hour clock, so 16.00 was not always understood or used. Before they returned, it was an afternoon in Bologna. Their first problem had been to leave their cases and then they had immediately, luckily, caught a shuttle bus.

It was very hot, so Francesca abandoned her idea of shopping and spent her afternoon in a friendly café near the bus station reading a guide book about Scotland which she had bought before leaving home. The café owner was a friendly lady who told Francesca that she had worked in London for a couple of years, but had never been to the north.

Have you been to this Watford Gap place? Francesca asked. *I keep seeing the name so it must be important, but when I look on the map there is nothing there. Only a small service station on the M1 motorway going north.*

The lady laughed. *It's a cultural thing. Many people in the south east of England go for holidays in America, Spain, Greece, France or other countries - but many don't go north. It's a foreign land to them. So there is a joke about needing a visa to pass the frontier at Watford Gap- which I think is only about 30 miles north of London. So where are you going?*

Somewhere near a place called Inverness I think. It's a long way north. It's in Scotland.

Ah. The land of the monster.

What monster? What do you mean? Francesca demanded.

You need to do some more reading. There is supposed to be a monster in the lake near Inverness. And the Scots call their lakes lochs, so it's called The Loch Ness Monster. So you are flying to Manchester or Glasgow tonight?

Francesca laughed. *No, my Dad made a mistake with the flight. We are arriving (1) in Gatwick and then driving to Scotland. (2)*

Not tonight I hope! The lady exclaimed. *Does he have any idea how far that is? Try to persuade him to stay somewhere overnight in a hotel.*

Francesca didn't reply. She had already gathered *(3)* that her Dad's company was not doing very well and didn't want him to feel obliged to spend any more money than necessary.

Meanwhile Pietro had found what he thought was a *lovely* bar a few streets away from Francesca and by the time the family met to catch the shuttle back to the airport he had wasted both time and money on a bottle of cheap wine which gave him a terrible headache. Lucia and Enrico had spent their time constructively in one of Bologna's many art galleries and had finished the afternoon with an excellent coffee and cake in a tiny café next to one of the galleries. They were in an excellent mood until they saw Pietro staggering *(4)* towards them, but they said nothing to avoid a public argument and sat quietly on the shuttle.

I don't believe it! Lucia exclaimed when they entered the terminal building.

…………………………………..

Grammar and Language Use

(1). **We are arriving in Gatwick and then driving north.** The present continuous is used here to communicate a clear plan for the future. This is a very common usage such as in

I am going *to my sister's party on Saturday.*

I am meeting *some friends tonight.*

We are going *to Spain for our holiday next year.*

(2). Some people would write / say *We are arriving in Gatwick and then we are driving north.* This repetition of *are* is not necessary because it is understood from the first part of the sentence.

But some teachers like to see this more traditional and formal use. There is an old expression: *When in Rome, do as the Romans.* The modern version is: *When in class do as the teacher – they may mark your exam paper.*

(3). **She had already *gathered*…** In this context ***gathered*** means to understand /know/ believe. **Not** to collect as in *He **gathered** some flowers from the garden and put them in a vase on the table.*

Some examples:

I **gather** from the forecast that it is going to snow tomorrow.

I **gather** that Mr Snowdon expected to be promoted but he was disappointed.

Yes, Amelia is very attractive but I **gather** she is already married.

I **gather** that the police think the car crashed because of a mechanical failure.

I **gather** from the press reports that the economy is growing at 2% a year.

(4). **they saw Pietro staggering towards them**. Pietro had drunk [Tenses: drink / drank / had drunk] too much and his parents could see this from the way he was walking. *Stagger* has other, useful meanings however, all of which are connected with some type of gap or pattern.

Some examples:

She borrowed some money from her parents to buy a car to get to university. By working in a bar at the weekend, she managed to save enough money to **stagger** *payments every second month. (So payments were made every second month).*

When they redecorated the bathroom, they chose a pattern of **staggered** *tiles: white, yellow, white, yellow, white, yellow and so on.*

He works for the fire service so he has to work shifts. There are 3 shifts, morning, afternoon and evening. Each of these is about 10 hours to allow for a change of shifts. The shifts are **staggered** *so that you never have to work a night shift followed by a morning shift.* [**Shift** is a useful word, so remember it.]

Comprehension and Vocabulary

1. What had Francesca originally planned to do? Why did she abandon her plan?

2. For how many years had the café owner lived in Britain? Why could she not help Francesca plan her holiday?

3. According to the café owner, why was Francesca surprised to hear about the monster?

4. *Not tonight I hope!* The lady exclaimed. Why did the café owner react in this way?

5. Where did Pietro spend his afternoon? [Think carefully about the tense changes in the verb *to spend*].

6. What was the difference in the ways Pietro and his parents had spent their afternoon?

7. Which aspect of Pietro's behaviour suggested to his parents that he had drunk too much.

Answers

1. Francesca had originally planned to do some shopping but she abandoned this plan because it was too hot.

2. The café owner had lived in Britain for a couple of years, but she had lived in London and had never been to Scotland.

3. The café owner thought Francesca was surprised to hear about the monster because she hadn't done enough reading about Scotland.

4. The café owner was shocked at the idea of the family driving from Gatwick to Scotland at the end of the day. She thought that they didn't understand the distance between the two areas.

5. Pietro had spent his afternoon drinking wine in a café.

6. *Lucia and Enrico had spent their time constructively...* This is a matter of personal judgment, but getting drunk before a flight is probably very unwise and perhaps not the best use of

money. By contrast, his parents had been to an art gallery and had enjoyed their *excellent* cake and coffee with no hangover to follow.

7. Pietro was staggering when he approached the bus terminus.

Episode Seven

Another hiccup *(1)*

I don't believe it! Lucia exclaimed when   they entered the terminal building.

What's wrong Mum?! Francesca demanded immediately, and then she saw the reason on the Departures screen. *Oh no. Not another delay. Is this day ever going to end?*

Pietro looked briefly at the screen before announcing in a quiet voice *I desperately need the loo (2)* and he suddenly found an increase in speed as he headed towards the nearest Gents'*(3)*.

That'll teach him, Mr Pasquati said without sympathy. *Drinking too much in this heat. And before flying. What an idiot.*

He'll learn, his wife agreed, though with more sympathy in her voice. *You two go and get the cases and I'll wait here for Pietro.*

It was about ten minutes later that the four were finally together again. Pietro still looked very much worse for wear *(4)* but he told his parents that he was going to be fine and so the family repeated their journey through check-in, security, passport control and finally arrived at the departure gate for their flight.

The area was empty except for a few, fixed, uncomfortable, chairs and there were no staff to handle *(5)* embarkation. *We came through too early. We should have stayed where there are shops* Pietro moaned. Before his parents could reply the helpful attendant from the morning suddenly emerged from a door marked **NO ENTRY. STAFF ONLY.**

You are back early, the lady they had met in the morning said cheerfully. *My colleague told me he got you sorted. (6)* She had a light coat draped over one arm and was carrying a large carrier bag from one of the local supermarkets.

Going home? Lucia asked with a grateful smile.

Yes, my shift started at six this morning, so it's been a long day. Thankfully I have tomorrow off, but it's always a pleasure dealing with your husband. He is such a gentleman compared with some of our customers.

Gentleman? Pietro was about to say more, but stopped when he saw the look on his parents' faces.

Many thanks for your help this morning, Lucia replied. *And for sorting things out so that we didn't have to pay for the new flight. That was very kind of you. By any chance do you know why the 18.00 flight is delayed?*

I think there was a hiccup with the luggage in London, the lady *(7)* replied. *Somebody checked in their luggage but then decided not to fly. So they had to remove her luggage from the hold. It happens occasionally.*

But I must go. My boyfriend is taking me out tonight. We've been together for a year now, so he's taking me for a meal at our favourite restaurant.

Thanks again, Lucia replied.

And have a good evening Laura! Enrico added as the lady walked away.

Laura? Francesca demanded. *How do you know her name?*

You father is not stupid Francesca, Lucia replied laughing. *He can read and she has a large name tag. And I think that he probably lived here when business was booming (8)*

Grammar and Vocabulary

(1). **Another hiccup** Physically, hiccup is singhiozzo, hoquet, hipo, Schluckauf. (I'm sorry if I haven't included your language). Here, the meaning of **hiccup** is that of a small problem.

For example: *There was a hiccup when we arrived at the hotel because they couldn't find our reservation to start.*

(2) and (3). **Loo** This is a very polite term for the toilet. *WC* is often used on signs, but people don't normally use this orally. *Loo, Gent's toilets, Ladies' Toilets, Gents' Ladies', Facilities, Men's, Women's* are also used. Young people may use the American *Rest Rooms.*

Note the use of the possessive with *Gents' and Ladies'* because these toilets belong to gents or ladies. *Men's, Women's* is becoming unusual.

You may hear *Bog.* **This is very vulgar** so <u>do not</u> use it.

(4) **worse for wear** Somebody, or something, is not in their best condition. Examples: *Our cat came in first thing this morning. He was very much* **worse for wear.** *It had been raining heavily all night and I don't think he had found a dry place to shelter.*

The car had done over 80,000 miles and was clearly **worse for wear.** *It had a lot of bumps and the owners had clearly not looked after it. So, she decided not to buy it.*

(5) **To handle.** In this situation *handle* means to arrange, organise, or deal with (manage) a problem.

(6) **sorted.** *Sorted* usually means to put in order, to put in the correct place. Here, it is used to mean to solve a problem.

Note how to handle and to sort can be used (sometimes together):

When the mail arrives in the morning my mother **sorts** *it and leaves the letters for my father on the table in the hall.*

A Mail Sorting Office (British Royal Mail Service)

There was a huge problem at work today, but my boss knew how to **handle** *it and it was soon* **sorted.**

My email software automatically **sorts** *the junk mail from my personal messages.*

I had a problem with my Internet connection this morning, but my friend Susanna knows a lot about computers and she **sorted** *the problem in minutes.*

Our computer is very old and cannot **handle** *much data. Trying to stream films is more than it can* **handle***.*

We had an angry dog running up and down our street, but our neighbour is really good at **handling** *animals and she managed to calm it down.*

(7). Notice the use of the term *lady*. *Woman* is less socially acceptable and *girl* can be insulting unless you are sure that the person is under 11 or you are their parent or teacher. In most schools you are a girl until later – perhaps around 16.

(8). when business was booming. When a business is *booming* its sales and profit are high.

Comprehension and Vocabulary

Remember to write your answers, or think about them, in full sentences.

1. Why was Francesca upset when they entered the terminal building?

2. Why were Mr and Mrs Pasquati angry with Pietro?

3. What was wrong with the area around the departure gate?

4. Why was the family's flight to London delayed? *[Remember to use the correct tenses.]*

5. Laura said '*…it's always a pleasure dealing with your husband. He is such a gentleman compared with some of our customers.'*

Why do you think she could say this in this situation?

6. Laura had 4 reasons to be cheerful. What were they?

7. Using all the information from this section, what do you learn about Mr Pasquati?

What Has Changed?

A reminder that careful reading is always important.

Here is a copy of some of the original section. There are 11 changes and /or deliberate mistakes (7 changes and 4 mistakes). How many can you find? It is always useful to read carefully, especially in a new leanguage.*

*Did you see that mistake?

I don't believe it! were Lucia's first words as they entered the terminal building.

What's wrong Mum?! Francesca demanded immediately, and then saw the reason on the Departures screen. *Oh no. Another delay. Is this day ever going to end?*

Pietro looked at the screen before announcing in a quiet voice *I desperately need the toilet* and he suddenly increased speed as he headed towards the nearest Gents'.

That will teach him, Mr Pasquati said without sympathy. *Drinking too much in this heat. And before flying. What an idiot!*

He'll learn his wife agreed, though with more sympathy in her voice. *You two go and get the cases and I'll wait here for Pietro.*

It was about ten minutes later that the four were finally together again. Pietro still looked very much worse for were but he told his parents that he was going to be fine and so the family repeated there journey through check-in, security, passport control and finally arrived at the departure gate for their flight.

The area was empty except for a few, fixed, uncomfortable chairs and there where no staff to handle embarkation. *We came through too early. We should have stayed where there were shops* Pietro moaned. Before his parents could reply the helpful attendant from the mourning suddenly emerged from a door marked **NO ENTRY. STAFF ONLY**.

You are back early, she said cheerfully. *My colleague told me he got you all sorted.* She had a light coat draped over one arm and was carrying a large carrier bag from one of the local supermarkets.

Going home? Lucia asked with a grateful smile.

Yes, my shift started at six this morning, so it's been a long day. Thankfully I have tomorrow off, but it's always a pleasure dealing with your husband. He is such a gentlemen compared with some of our customers.

> If you are asking yourself the purpose of this exercise, it was to encourage attention to detail and careful observation and the ability to be precise and concentrate. These are essential skills in exams and in work environments.

Answers

1. Francesca was upset because she saw that the flight had been delayed. Also, she was frustrated that this was another delay [*Is this day ever going to end?*]

2. Mr and Mrs Pasquati were angry with Pietro because he had drunk too much.

You could also say that *Mr and Mrs Pasquati were angry with Pietro because he was drunk.*

3. The area around the departure gate was empty except for a few, fixed, uncomfortable chairs and totally empty [*there were no staff to handle embarkation*].

In addition, the area had no shops and so Pietro felt that they had come through too early and may have wanted something from the shops. [*We came through too early. We should have stayed where there are shops* Pietro moaned].

4. The flight from London had been delayed because a passenger's luggage had been loaded in the aircraft's hold but then the passenger had decided not to fly.

5. She could praise Mr Pasquati because there was only his family in the area at the time and no other customers.

6. Laura was cheerful because her shift was ending, she had the following day off work, she was going for a meal with her boyfriend at their favourite restaurant and it was their anniversary.

She also seemed pleased that her colleagues had *got you all sorted* and she enjoyed dealing with Mr Pasquati [*it's always a pleasure dealing with your husband. He is such a gentleman compared with some of our customers.*]

So you may argue that she had 6 reasons for being cheerful.

7. The extract suggests that Mr Pasquati:

a). Is not sympathetic towards Pietro [*That'll teach him* Mr Pasquati decided with no sympathy. *Drinking too much in this heat. And before flying. What an idiot.*]

b) Is a polite, reasonable person when dealing with the airline staff [*'…it's always a pleasure dealing with your husband. He is such a gentleman compared with some of our customers.'*]

c). Is attentive to some details: [*You father is not stupid Francesca* Lucia replied laughing. *He can read and she has a large name tag.*]

d). Was a regular customer at the airport at one time, but his business is not so good now [*And I think that he probably lived here when business was booming.*]

Answers to What Has Changed?

Here is a copy of some of the original section.

There are some changes and deliberate mistakes. How many can you find?

I don't believe it! Lucia exclaimed as they entered the terminal building.

What's wrong Mum?! Francesca demanded immediately, and then saw the reason on the Departures screen. *Oh no.* **Not IS MISSING** *Another delay. Is this day ever going to end?* **[CHANGE 1]**

Pietro looked **briefly *IS MISSING*** at the screen before announcing in a quiet voice *I desperately need the **loo** **replaced by** **toilet** and '**he suddenly found an increase in speed'** **was the original** he suddenly increased speed* as he headed towards the nearest Gents'. **[CHANGES 2, 3, 4]**

That will **That'll was the original** *teach him,* Mr Pasquati said without sympathy. *Drinking too much in this heat. And before flying. What an idiot*** ! No exclamation mark in the original. [CHANGES 5 and 6]**

He'll learn his wife agreed, though with more sympathy in her voice. *You two go and get the cases and I'll wait here for Pietro.*

It was about ten minutes later that the four were finally together again. Pietro still looked very much worse for were **worse for wear is the correct, original. [MISTAKE 1 Spelling]** but he told his parents that he was going to be fine and so the family repeated there **This should be their the possessive because it is their journey. 'There' is for place and time.** their journey through check-in, security, passport control and finally arrived at the departure gate for their flight. **[MISTAKE 2 Spelling]**

The area was empty except for a few, fixed, uncomfortable chairs and there **where [MISTAKE 3 Spelling] [This should be were simple past of verb to be; where is an adverb used in questions and refers to location]** no staff to handle embarkation. *We came through too early. We should have stayed where there were* **are was the original** *shops* Pietro moaned. **[CHANGE 7]** Before his parents could reply the helpful attendant from the mourning suddenly emerged from a door marked ***NO ENTRY. STAFF ONLY.***

You are back early, she said cheerfully. *My colleague told me he got you all sorted.* She had a light coat draped over one arm and was carrying a large carrier bag from one of the local supermarkets.

Going home? Lucia asked with a grateful smile.

Yes, my shift started at six this morning, so it's been a long day. Thankfully I have tomorrow off, but it's always a pleasure dealing with your husband. He is such a gentlemen **gentleman is correct and was in the original** *compared with some of our customers.* **[MISTAKE 4 Spelling]**

Episode Eight

Finally- take off

This section is full of useful terms. Some teachers might say there are too many, but this is a realistic section- I didn't invent English!

The family had been sitting for about *(1)* twenty minutes when the next passengers arrived. Then, a few *(2)* minutes later, a couple of people from the service company suddenly appeared to re-check *(3)* the boarding passes. Lucia hadn't flown for a few years, *(2)* and had been accustomed to the slower speed of the major airlines, so she was a bit shocked by the speed with which they were ushered *(4)* onto the stairs leading down to the exit onto the tarmac. They stood there for some *(1)* ten minutes before the doors were opened and they walked down and out towards the waiting aircraft.

Enrico. I'm sure I remember a system where you walked through a covered tunnel to the aircraft Mrs Pasquati observed to her husband. It had started to drizzle *(5)* and Lucia hated getting wet.

Economies, love (6). All the airlines are trying to save money and that costs them more in airport charges. Didn't you notice that the two who re-checked our tickets were the same as the ones at the check-in? I suspect the older one will be the pilot.

Mrs Pasquati stopped abruptly. *You are joking. I know I'm getting to the age when the police look too young to be out of school, but how could she have a pilot's licence?*

I'm joking her husband laughed. *But you are right. Everyone is starting to look so young - which means that we are probably starting to look old.*

Yes. And everyone is starting to get wet. So can you two move, Pietro demanded. His father gave him a disapproving look but said nothing, and a few minutes later they had boarded the aircraft and stowed *(7)* their hand luggage above their seats. The aircraft was half empty, so finding empty stowage space was not a problem. The cabin crew were clearly in a hurry to make up for the delay, and dashed *(8)* back and forward in the cabin trying to get the passengers seated, their luggage safely stowed and seat belts fastened.

Then there was the statutory *(9)* information about seat belts, escape routes, life jackets, lights during take-off and landing, and not smoking in the toilets. Finally, there was a brief greeting from the pilot before a sudden jolt as the aircraft was pulled backwards into its position on the runway. The noise from the engines increased and then they bumped along the runway, increased speed and finally left the ground and climbed steeply into the sky. *Finally!* Francesca declared. *I thought we would never leave.* Almost immediately the aircraft turned quickly to their right but then there was a jolt as they met some turbulence and they dropped in height. Francesca's *(10)* face filled with alarm as Pietro's *(10)* face turned a bright green. *Mum! Dad!* She almost shouted to her parents who were sitting on the other side of the aisle *(11)*. *Pietro is being sick!*

Francesca, give him that plastic bag you had your books in, Mrs Pasquati said urgently. *And Pietro, once these seat belt lights go off I want you to go to the toilets and clean yourself up(11). And apologise to the cabin crew for the mess you've made. You should be ashamed of yourself (11).*

Grammar and Vocabulary

(1). About is used here to mean approximately/ around that amount of time.

(2). few. Notice how flexible this word is. *A few seconds* may perhaps be up to a minute.

A few minutes? Perhaps up to ten, though cultures differ on this. A few minutes late for an Italian may perhaps be up to 20 – for a German it may be 5 or 10. In Britain, it may perhaps be up to 15- but not for a business meeting.

A few years? A few centuries? These are very variable. A historian might talk about *a few centuries* as covering hundreds of years.

(3). re-check here means to check again. *Re* is commonly used with the meaning of *do again / repeat.*

Some examples: *The teacher told Louis that his work was so bad that he had to **re-do** it.*

*I failed my university exams last year, but I am **re-applying** and **re-taking** all of the subjects.*

*They did such a bad job painting the room that my father told them to **re-paint** it.*

Be careful not to confuse this with composite words such as replace, refund, return, reseal.

(4) to usher has a formal meaning of 'to lead' / 'to show' to the right place. It is not widely used for people, but is used as a verb. Some countries have ushers in cinemas, theatres and in weddings.

Some examples:

*It was a very formal restaurant, and we were **ushered** to our table by the head waiter.*

*We arrived late at the cinema and the **usher** showed us to our seats. She had a small torch to show us the way.*

*When we arrived at the church the **ushers** showed us to our seats. The friends and relatives of the bride were on one side of the aisle and the friends and relatives of the groom on the other side of the aisle.*

(5). drizzle a slight, fine rain. The word is now often used in restaurants and cafes to describe a small amount of sauce, flavoured/spicy powder or alcohol added to the surface of a meal, drink, ice cream etc.

(6). Economies, love. There are two ideas here. *Economies* is a short way for Mr Pasquati to say that the airline company is saving money by using staff to do many different things at work.

Love is, of course, a term of great affection and this is how Mr Pasquati is using it when speaking to his wife.

However, *luv* (which has exactly the same pronunciation, or luvie which is more used in the north) is widely used in Britain as a greeting, especially in informal situations. It is especially used by men when speaking to women, between women and by older women towards children and young adolescents. So, *Where are you trying to get to luv?* at the railway station, or *What can I get you luv?* by a waitress in a café is OK.

Hello luv said by a stranger is not OK.

(7). To stow is to put things away in an ordered way. It is usually used on aircraft, boats/ships and by the military.

(8). To dash To run or move quickly

(9). statutory required by law (by statute)

(10). Francesca's face / Pietro's face. Note the use of the possessive here. The *face of Francesca* is not a normal structure.

(11). Aisle. You met this in point 4 where it described the division of seats in a church. The same term is used for the seating on an aircraft. *When we arrived at the church the* **ushers** *showed us to our seats. The friends and relatives of the bride were on one side of the* **aisle** *and the friends and relatives of the groom on the other side of the* **aisle***.*

(12). clean yourself up. And apologise to the cabin crew for the mess you've made. You should be ashamed of yourself. Note the use of the reflexive verbs here. We shall have some more examples of this later.

Comprehension

1. Why did Mrs Pasquati suddenly stop on the tarmac?

2. What reason did Mr Pasquati give for the change in the boarding system at the airport?

3. Why were the cabin crew dashing around in the cabin?

4. Why was Pietro sick?

Word Search

Here is some vocabulary from the sections you have already read. Find the 21 words and ensure that you understand them. **They may be vertical, horizontal, diagonal or reversed.** *When you have found the words, why not try using them in a sentence and discussing with a friend if your use is correct?*

usher   moan   hiccup   stow   pastry   plate   gather   tray   shuttle
security   clear   cashier   purse   aisle   choked   stagger   loo   handle
gentleman   turbulence

```
R  J  J  P  K  M  T  R  A  Y  V  A  E  W  F  P  J
I  T  O  A  P  L  F  M  P  E  M  G  O  S  E  W  Z
M  E  Y  C  I  X  Q  R  J  O  H  A  T  O  R  G  V
W  R  L  R  I  S  A  Z  A  B  Y  L  Z  J  L  U  K
Y  M  E  F  T  U  N  O  C  L  E  A  R  K  U  P
X  R  C  D  I  S  O  E  U  S  T  O  W  D  G  T  U
T  E  N  P  D  I  A  Y  R  E  H  S  U  Q  F  R  E
W  H  E  B  O  U  G  P  I  K  U  G  C  Y  L  T  Y
G  T  L  G  G  F  B  B  T  I  L  G  R  Q  A  T  W
E  A  U  K  S  H  I  C  C  U  P  D  A  L  U  Q  O
N  G  B  K  E  L  T  T  U  H  S  T  P  D  O  B  L
T  F  R  S  E  E  L  D  N  A  H  H  I  L  D  R  U
L  Q  U  L  C  Q  T  Q  Y  S  T  A  G  G  E  R  X
E  C  T  A  C  H  O  K  E  D  Z  Z  M  U  I  R  M
M  V  K  C  A  S  H  I  E  R  M  Z  N  G  M  F  J
A  T  I  G  L  E  R  M  Q  B  H  I  F  U  R  Q  U
N  H  P  Y  T  I  R  U  C  E  S  P  Y  V  M  M  I
```

Answers

1. Mrs Pasquati suddenly stopped because her husband had told her that the very young person was the pilot.

2. Mr Pasquati thought that the changes had happened because the airlines were trying to save money.

3. The cabin crew were in a hurry because the flight had arrived late.

4. Pietro was sick because he had drunk too much and because of the sudden movements of their aircraft.

Word Search Answers

usher   moan   hiccup   stow   pastry

plate   gather   tray   shuttle   security   clear

cashier   purse   aisle   choked   stagger

loo   handle   gentleman   turbulence

Episode Nine

Gatwick

You smell terrible Pietro, Francesca said loudly. The family was standing at the end of the queue for Passport Control and were trying to stay away from the other passengers.

This is so embarrassing, Mrs Pasquati hissed (1), trying to hide behind Francesca. *The lady with the white blouse is Mrs Bauer.*

Who? Pietro queried.

You know. The German lady from Berlin who lives two floors down from us. I sometime go for a coffee with her during the week if her husband and your Dad are away. I don't know what I'll say to her when we next meet.

Say it was food poisoning, Pietro mumbled.

Food poisoning with a smell of red wine, Mr Pasquati replied. *But it's even worse (2). That tall man with the red hair is an executive from one of the companies I sometime work with here in London. What a disaster. You have disgraced the entire family Pietro.*

I … Pietro started but then decided that there really was no point in arguing.

Once we've collected our luggage from the carousels, I'm going to open your case and you can go into the toilets and change your clothes, his mother instructed. *I'll give you a plastic bag to put your dirty clothes in. We can decide what to do with them later, but make sure you seal the bag well. We don't want that smell all the way north.*

Pietro said nothing, but nodded his head. He had a terrible headache and knew he had behaved badly, but was also feeling miserable because he really did not want to be on this holiday. Originally, he had willingly agreed to come, but that was before he had met Michele and got involved in the new game - *The best game on the planet* they had both agreed. And then, a month earlier, he had met Françoise, a French girl with lovely blue eyes and blonde hair. Pietro had immediately fallen in love, so now he wanted to be with her on a hot beach instead of going to this silly place which his Mum had warned him was like a fridge even in summer.

The Passport Control at Gatwick was busy, but quite efficient, and within ten minutes they had passed through and found their luggage was already indicated for collection from the carousels. They were waiting for this to start delivering the cases when there was a double disaster. *Lucia, what a surprise. What are you doing here? I thought you were going to Scotland. Not London* Mrs Bauer declared with a huge smile and she stepped forward to give her neighbour a friendly hug. Unfortunately Pietro was standing next to his mother and there was a clear look of surprise on Mrs Bauer's face when she saw the mess on Pietro's clothes.

Mrs Pasquati was saved by the carousel suddenly lurching into action and her own case appearing. *So lovely to see you* she lied. *But that's my case and we are already late. Technical Problems with an earlier flight,* she lied again. *I'll explain everything when we meet for a coffee when we get back. Sorry, I must go.* And she dashed off to help Francesca who was struggling to pull her Mum's heavy case from the carousel.

What's wrong with Dad? Francesca asked, and Mrs Pasquati realised for the first time that her husband was not looking for their cases but was standing, shaking his head and looking at a slip of paper he was holding in his hand. She quickly walked over to her husband.

What's wrong now? She demanded.

I've just realised that I booked the flight but my secretary booked the car Mr Pasquati replied miserably. *She was more efficient than me, so she actually booked the hire car from Stansted and here we are at Gatwick. I just hope that they have a spare car here.*

A Map of the London area showing the position of the main airports.

Grammar and Vocabulary

1. This is so embarrassing Mrs Pasquati **hissed** (1). Some snakes **hiss** when angry and in humans the word is used to describe when people speak with anger, and usually quietly, to avoid others hearing. It is also used to try and silence other. Some examples:

This is an exam and you are not allowed to talk, so please stop immediately the teacher **hissed**.

Can you two please stop talking. All my customers are trying to enjoy this film and you are disturbing them, the cinema manager **hissed.**

Wait until they are a bit closer. Then we'll come out from behind this wall and arrest the thieves the police sergeant **hissed** to his team.

2. it's **even** *worse.* **Even** is an adverb used to show and emphasise surprise, an unexpected/ extreme event or action. It is often used in front of a comparative as in this example.

For Mrs Pasquati, meeting her neighbour was bad, but her husband saw the possible loss of work. When used in this way **even** is clearly negative.

Some examples:

We had so much work this week that we **even** had to work all of the weekend.

They stayed with us the entire week but didn't **even** thank us before they left.

That customer was really difficult but he didn't **even** leave a tip for the staff.

I felt very cold **even though*** I was wearing a very heavy coat. [* This is a common combination expressing surprise about a negative event or situation.]

Even though the hotel had good reviews the quality was poor.

I failed my exams **even though** I had worked hard.

Or you may prefer this?

I passed my exams **even though** I had done no work.

Comprehension

1. Why was Mrs Pasquati trying to hide?

2. Why did Mr Pasquati say *But it's even worse?*

3. What do we learn about Mrs Bauer from this passage?

4. In what way did the carousel *save* Mrs Pasquati?

5. Why was there a problem with the hire car?

Answers

1. Mrs Pasquati was trying to hide behind Francesca because she had seen Mrs Bauer, one of her neighbours. This was an embarrassing situation because they had landed at the wrong airport and Pietro had been sick on his clothes during the flight.

2. Mr Pasquati thought that the situation was *even worse* because he had seen someone he did business with. For him, this was more embarrassing and more important than meeting the neighbour.

3. Mrs Bauer comes from Berlin in Germany, she lives two floors down from the Pasquatis and her husband goes away for work. When Mr Bauer and Mr Pasquati and both away, their wives sometimes go for a coffee together during the week. She smiled at Mrs Pasquati and was about to hug her, so the two ladies were quite friendly. That evening, at the airport, Mrs Pasquati was wearing a white blouse.

4. Mrs Pasquati was embarrassed by Pietro's state and by the fact that the family had landed at the wrong airport. She did not want to explain things, so when the carousel started and her suitcase arrived she had an excuse to stop the conversation with Mrs Bauer and help Francesca with the case. She promised to explain things when they next met for a coffee.

5. Mr Pasquati had booked the flight tickets and these were to a different airport from the airport where his secretary had booked the hire car. It was possible that the hire company didn't have a car.

Episode Ten
Car Hire at Gatwick- a difficult experience

Grammar: When reading this section, look carefully at how the story switches between past continuous, past perfect and past simple.

From now, the work uses the normal, informal form of the past perfect e.g. *I'd* rather than *I had.* **Remember to use the formal structure if your teachers or examination system require this.**

Car Hire at Gatwick

Once all the family's cases had come off the carousel, Mr. Pasquati quickly lead the family downstairs to the area where the car hire companies were located. He'd flown to Gatwick many times for business and knew exactly where the desk was located. He was hoping that he would know the staff on duty and they would do him a favour by changing his booking from Stansted to Gatwick.

He was disappointed to see a young woman at the desk. She was not someone he knew. *Hiya!* She declared cheerfully when he arrived at the desk. Mr Pasquati stopped. He was puzzled by what he thought was the question.

Yes, that is what you do, hire cars, he replied. It was the woman's turn to look puzzled.

Yes, she said slowly. She was still puzzled. *We hire cars. We don't sell them. Last year we did have a rich foreign customer who wanted to buy one, but the company doesn't do that. So, how can I help you? You want to hire a car?*

I've already hired a car, Mr. Pasquati replied quickly *but it's in the wrong place.*

Ah. I understand the woman replied, but she was still looking puzzled. *So you'd hired one of our cars and now you want to return it, but you've parked it in the wrong place. Is that right? Where did you park it?*

Let me explain from the beginning, Mr Pasquati replied, trying to be patient. *My secretary booked a car with your company, but she booked it for Stansted airport and we have arrived here, at Gatwick.*

Really? Was there an emergency, were you diverted? The woman demanded. She was now more interested and excited.

No, there was … and he stopped. He was too embarrassed to explain his mistake.

My husband's secretary made a mistake with the reservation Mrs Pasquati explained. The family was already tired and she wanted to avoid more delays. *The reservation is in the name of Pasquati. That's p.a.s.q.u.a.t.i.*

Like Easter the woman replied cheerfully. *I studied Italian at uni. University. Let me see what I can do,* she said, looking at her screen. *I love Italy. I studied both Italian and French. I was lucky. I had a placement in both Florence and Lyon. Ah yes, here you are. I've found your booking on our system. But, I'm sorry. I can transfer the booking to this office, but we don't have a car of the size you need – 4 people and 4 large cases? Yes?*

Oh no. Not another problem Francesca moaned and Pietro unwisely shook his head which was still hurting.

What are we going to do then Enrico? Mrs Pasquati asked unhappily.

If it helps, I can get a car ready for you for around eight thirty tomorrow morning and I have a friend who works at the airport's Premier Inn. There's one at the North Terminal. They are usually quite reasonable (1). Do you want me to see if they have availability? You folks do look a bit tired, especially the young man. So a good night's sleep and an early start might be a good idea. Are you going far?

Scotland Francesca replied immediately. *At this rate we'll arrive in the next couple of years.*

Scotland? Then you do need to get some rest. You are going the long way from here. Stansted is much better. But do you want me to see if there is still availability.

Please. Mr Pasquati sighed. *This has not been a good start to the holiday.*

Grammar and Vocabulary

(1) *Quite reasonable.* Reasonable is used here to describe a price or quality. It is a way to avoid saying that something is cheap or expensive. *[Saying something is cheap is unwise. It either means that the seller does not understand the market and is selling at too low a price or that the quality is bad.]*

Some examples of use:
The price the garage charged for repairing the car was very **reasonable**.
We paid over £300 when our central heating system broke down. I thought it was a lot, but my wife thought it was a very **reasonable** charge because the plumber came at 11 o'clock on Christmas Eve.
Our new carpet is expensive, but the quality is very good and there is a 10 year guarantee. So, it is actually a **reasonable** price.

Comprehension Questions (Read carefully! Things can be tricky.)

1. Why was Mr Pasquati so familiar with the location of the car hire desk?

2. What was the problem with Mr Pasquati's car hire reservation?

3. Why was the woman at the desk not totally confused during her conversation with Mr Pasquati?

4. Where had Mr Pasquati parked his car?

5. Why did the woman think that the family was at the wrong airport?

6. What skills or knowledge did the woman have that might have helped the family?

7. What was the formal link between the hotel at the airport and the woman at the car hire desk?

8. What was the informal link between the hotel at the airport and the woman at the car hire desk?

A Quick Knowledge Test

Why is this section important? Language contains many words which provide a context and help understanding. For example, the names Conte or Salvini provide a context in relation to history or politics, Tiber or Po to geography.

It is easy to fail to understand a sentence, especially oral sentences, if they contain unknown names. Doing some research, especially if you do it in English, will improve your English skills.

So, when talking about Britain:

1. Britain can also be described as GB which means............ , or the UK which means........?
2. Normally, people say that the UK has 4 nations. These are....................................?
3 Manx is the name for which island which is semi-independent from the British government?
4. The capital of Wales is ....?
5. What is the name given to the area in London which describes the national government?
6. The capital of England is..........?
7. Ulster is the name sometimes used to describe which part of the United Kingdom?
8. The capital of the Republic of Ireland (RoI) is............?
9. The capital of Northern Ireland is.............?
10. The capital of Scotland is ....?

Answers

1. Mr Pasquati was very familiar with the location of the car hire desk at Gatwick Airport because he had flown there on business several time.

2. The problem with Mr Pasquati's car hire reservation was that his secretary had reserved the car at Stansted Airport and Mr Pasquati had booked flights to Gatwick.

3. The woman at the desk was not totally confused because she'd already had an experience of a customer trying to buy a car from her car hire company.

4. Mr Pasquati had parked <u>his</u> car at Bologna Airport that morning. **His** is the key word here.

5. The woman thought that their flight had been diverted for some reason- perhaps an emergency.

6. The woman had a knowledge of Italian and had also lived in Italy.

7. There is no evidence that there was a **formal** link between the hotel at the airport and the woman at the car hire desk.

8. The **informal** link was that the woman at the car hire desk had a friend who worked at the hotel.

*[**Cultural note:** In Britain, informal links are often not very useful because many systems are controlled centrally by computers.]*

Answers to a Quick Knowledge Test

1. Britain can also be described as GB which means Great Britain, or the UK which means United Kingdom.
2. Normally, people say that the UK has 4 nations. These are England, Wales, Scotland and Northern Ireland.
3. The Isle of Man.
4. The capital of Wales is Cardiff.
5. Westminster.
6. Trick Question. England does not have an official capital. The national capital is London.
7. Northern Ireland.
8. Dublin.
9. Stormont /Belfast. Both terms are used. Stormont is an area, which people talk about like Westminster. Belfast is the city. People often talk about Westminster when they mean the government of the UK and Stormont when they mean the government of Northern Ireland.
10. The capital of Scotland is Edinburgh.

Episode Eleven

Breakfast

This section is used to revise grammar and develop reported speech. Reported speech is important when describing conversations, and being able to report conversations accurately is an important skill. It is not very easy because it requires a good understanding of verbs and tenses.

Consequently, even if you think you will never need to report a conversation, this is a useful skill to develop. If you find it hard now, do not worry. We shall work on this several times.

………………………………..

Good Morning! Have you booked breakfast? Can I please have your room numbers? It was seven thirty and the young woman at the entrance to the hotel's restaurant was clearly in a good mood. Perhaps it was the bright sunshine outside. The sunshine was puzzling Francesca who had never been to Britain before, but had an image of incessant rain as a result of watching too many Hollywood films.

Rooms 232 and 467, Mr Pasquati replied, trying to hide his fatigue. *We are four – my son is going to join us in a few minutes.*

No prob,(1) the woman replied. *So you've booked one Full English Breakfast and three Continentals (2). That's right? You know the prices are different? Have you been here before? If not, my colleague here can show you around.*

That's not necessary. I've been here before on business, Mr Pasquati replied. *I'd like some porridge (3). Can you organise that? And can we sit at that table next to the window?*

Certainly, the woman replied and she ushered the three to the table Mr Pasquati had indicated. *I'll order the porridge for you, sir. You've been here before, so I'll leave you to help yourselves.*

So how does it work Enrico? Mrs Pasquati demanded as soon as the girl was out of earshot (4). She was clearly only slightly older than Francesca, so for Mrs Pasquati she was definitely *a girl.*

We help ourselves, her husband replied. *The coffee, tea, juices etc. are there, it's coffee from the machine and hot water from the boiler for the tea – they usually have different types of tea. I ordered Full English so I'll help myself to the bacon, sausages, baked beans and eggs. There are cereals, rolls, jams and the like (5) on the counter around the corner. Is that OK? Just help yourselves. Can I get you girls (6) something to drink?*

Do they always eat so much for breakfast? Francesca demanded in amazement. *At home I just have an espresso and a couple of biscuits.*

I fear we are going to need to diet when we get back home, her Mum replied sympathetically, *but for now enjoy a good breakfast. Yesterday was not the best we've ever had.*

She was right. There had been the problem with her husband's passport which he had left at his office, then the terrible traffic on the way to the airport followed by the realisation that Mr Pasquati had booked for the wrong airport. Mrs Pasquati had actually enjoyed the unexpected time in Bologna. Her husband was often away for work and she had enjoyed the opportunity to share some time with him and view the paintings at the gallery. Then Pietro had spoilt things by getting so drunk that he had been sick on their flight, and finally there had been the issue of the car hire. At least Mr Pasquati had had the foresight (7) to go online and book rooms at the hotel, though they had managed to find only two instead of the three he had wanted.

How did you sleep? Her husband had returned with a plate piled with food and a couple of cups of coffee, one for each of them.

Well, Mrs Pasquati replied. *I hadn't looked forward to sharing a bed with Francesca, but needs must (8) and she fell asleep instantly. The poor girl was exhausted. And you?*

Badly, her husband replied. *Pietro is really being selfish. You know that when he went to the loos at the airport and changed out of his dirty clothes he didn't even bother to put them in a plastic bag? The room stank as soon as he opened his case. And he refused to share a bed with me. So he slept on that sofa by the window. And he woke me in the middle of the night. You know what he was doing at three in the morning? He was playing that stupid game online with Michele.*

You know he is going to try and ruin the holiday? Francesca asked. She had re-joined her parents and had followed her father's example by piling her plate full of food. There was muesli, yoghurt, bread, jam and some small croissants from the Continental Breakfast bar. *He wants to be back with his friend Michele and his mates (9) - and there is that new girl he really likes. The French one this time.*

What happened to Laura? Mr Pasquati asked. *I thought she was a nice girl.*

Perhaps too nice for Pietro, Francesca laughed. *And it's a different month, so for Pietro that means a different girl. But be careful, here he comes.*

Vocabulary and Culture

(1) No prob. **INFORMAL ENGLISH.** This is a shortened version of *no problem* or, as some travelled individuals may say- incorrectly- *no problemo*.

This imported expression is now used in many situations and can mean *I'm pleased to help you, I'll do that, I'll get it*. Personally, I find it strange when you offer to pay the bill, in a restaurant for example, and the waiter/waitress* tells you that there is no problem taking money from you. [*The American *server* is increasingly used.]

An example of use:

I'd like to pay please.

Yes, no prob. Cash or card?

(2) So you've booked one Full English Breakfast and three Continentals. Full English will normally include the offer of porridge, eggs, bacon, baked beans, tomatoes, hash brownies and toast. In Scotland, *Full Scottish Breakfast* may also offer fish and black and white pudding. Breakfast is an important meal in Britain and is often used to satisfy your hunger for much of the day.

(3) Porridge is a traditional breakfast food – especially in Scotland- made from oats. The oats are cooked on a low heat for a few minutes with a mixture of milk and water (usually 50/50). It can be eaten with milk or sugar, salt, jam, honey or yoghurt added [One- not all at the same time!!]. I've even seen bacon added!

(4) out of earshot. To be too far away to be able to hear something.

(5) and the like. Similar types of food.

(6) girls. Mr Pasquati is using this informal term to address his wife and daughter. Pietro is around 20, so that suggests that Mrs Pasquati is probably at least a 40 year old *girl* .

(7) foresight. The ability to think or plan in the future. [*Fore* is often used as part of words involving the future / ahead/ in front of. Look in your dictionary for the meaning of examples such as forehead, foresee, foretell, forecast, forewarn.]

(8) needs must. This is a fixed term used to communicate that the speaker must do something, but doesn't want to do it. Some examples:

I don't want to visit her family next week, **but needs must**. [*Why? Because there will be negative consequences if the person does not go.*]

She didn't want to wear trousers to the interview, but her friend said that the company expected it so, **needs must,** she bought a new pair of trousers.

My car had broken down, but I had to go to work. There was no bus service so, **needs must**, I went to work by bike in the pouring rain.

(9). Mates. Generally, mates are not as close as friends and the term is more often used by males than females. A simple hierarchy among males: *Close friend, friend, mates, matey, acquaintance, casual acquaintance, seen him/her around.*

Brother and bro are used by some - primarily young - parts of the population with West Indian or Asian origins. Occasionally it is used by young whites. **RECOGNISE, BUT DO NOT USE!**

Comprehension

1. Why did Francesca fall asleep immediately?

2. What was it about Francesca's first experience of Britain that puzzled her?

3. Who had stayed in room 237?

4. Why did Mrs Pasquati ask her husband about how things were organised for breakfast?

5. Why was Francesca so surprised about breakfast?

6. Why had Mr Pasquati slept badly?

7. What had Pietro done to upset Mr Pasquati?

Grammar Development

We are going to use the Pasquati's conversation to develop your skills in reported speech. Reported speech is used to communicate what has already been said or written. Some important points:

1. Traditionally, speech was indicated by speech marks " " or ' ' in the written form.

Note the comma [,] at the end of the direct speech.

An example: Henry said " I loved Copenhagen," when he talked about his summer holidays with his mates.

Many modern publications omit the " " marks and indicate speech using italics. This is the system I use.

An example: Henry said *I loved Copenhagen* when he talked about his summer holidays with his mates.

In reported speech we take Henry's words but we have to make some changes:

An example: Henry said **he** *[replaces I]* loved Copenhagen when **he** talked about **his** summer holidays with **his** mates.

2. Traditionally, and even today, many people used **that** as an indicator of reported speech. *[I suggest you use it until you are very confident because it will help you remember the rules.]*

An example: Henry said **that** he loved Copenhagen when he talked about his summer holidays with his mates.

3. In reported speech, we need to consider several things:

a). changing the pronoun. We did that with **he** and **I** in point 2.

b). deciding if what has been said needs to be changed.

For example: When I was young I shouted at my parents *I really hate this place we are staying in.*

The problems: I *[this is not you]*, my parents *[these are not your parents]*, this place *[you are no longer in the same place]*.

The speaker [or writer] explained / said / wrote that he /she shouted at his / her parents that he/ she really **hated** *[Notice this change. We discuss in point 5]* the place he / she **was staying** *[Notice this change. We discuss in point 5]*.

The finished version: The speaker said that she shouted at her parents that she really hated the place she was staying in.

4. There is *generally* a need to shift the verb one tense back. Some examples:

- *I am [present simple] 13* said Helen.

   Helen said that **she was** *[past simple]* 13.

[In modern English many people will say **Helen said that she is 13,** but this is not strictly correct according to users of traditional grammar.]

- *I **am waiting** for you [present continuous] at the station Tom.*

 Helen <u>explained</u> [note that this verb is unchanged].

Helen explained to Tom that **she was waiting** *[past continuous]* for him at the station.

- *I had been [past perfect] at the station for over an hour when Tom arrived,* Helen complained to her friend.

   <u>**There is no tense in the past after the past perfect, so the reported speech has to use the past perfect.**</u>

   Helen complained to her friend that she **had been** [past perfect] at the station for over an hour when Tom arrived.

- There is also the possibility of using the past perfect continuous. This describes a continuing event in the past followed by the past simple. If Helen **<u>feels</u>** that she waited a long time or was **<u>angry</u>** with Tom, she can use this.

   …………………………………………………………….... X

   The dots represent Helen waiting for over an hour and the **X the arrival of Tom.**

   Helen complained to her friend that **she had been waiting** [past perfect continuous] at the station for over an hour **when Tom arrived**.
   …………………………

<u>Let us see how this works with some conversations between Mr and Mrs Pasquati.</u>

- *So how does it work Enrico?* Mrs Pasquati demanded as soon as the girl was out of earshot.

This becomes:

As soon as the girl was out of earshot, Mrs Pasquati asked **her husband** how the system in the restaurant **worked.**

- *How did you sleep?* Her husband had returned with a plate piled with food and a couple of cups of coffee, one for each of them.

  Well, Mrs Pasquati replied. *I hadn't looked forward to sharing a bed with Francesca…*

This becomes:

When Mr Pasquati returned with a plate piled with food and a couple of cups of coffee, one for each of them, **he** asked **his** wife how **she had slept. She replied** that **she had slept well,** but **she hadn't looked forward** to sharing a bed with Francesca.

- *What happened to Laura?* Mr Pasquati asked. *I thought she was a nice girl. What happened with her?*

This becomes:

Mr Pasquati asked what **had happened** to Laura. **He said** that **he had thought** that **she was** a nice girl.

Practice

We shall come back to this topic again. For now, try to turn the following sentences into reported speech.

1. *You were travelling too fast,* the policeman claimed. [Note: you are not involved in this incident].

2. *Andrea has lost her purse,* Bill told Harry.

3. *I think it has rained a lot,* Henry said to Alan.

4. *My car has broken down and I need a mechanic,* Zoe explained to her breakdown service.

5. *I scored 100% in the maths test,* Will told his parents as soon as he got home.

Answers

Comprehension

1. Francesca fell asleep immediately because she was exhausted.

2. Francesca was puzzled because it was not raining. In all the Hollywood films she had seen it was raining incessantly in Britain.

3. We do not know the answer to this trick question. The Pasquati family had stayed in *Rooms 232 and 467.*

4. Mr Pasquati had stayed at this hotel before, so he knew how things worked at breakfast.

5. In Italy, Francesca had an expresso and a couple of biscuits for breakfast. She was surprised at the amount of food people were eating for breakfast at the hotel.

6. Mr Pasquati had slept badly because of the smell from Pietro's case and because Pietro woke him in the middle of the night when he was playing a game with Michele.

Practice Answers

1. The policeman claimed that the person had been travelling too fast. *[It could also be a bike rider or cyclist or simply person, but you need to identify who he was talking to.*

You were travelling too fast, the policeman claimed.

2. Bill told Harry that Andrea had lost her purse on the bus.

Andrea has lost her purse on the bus, Bill told Harry .

3. Henry said to Alan that he thought it had rained a lot.

I think it has rained a lot Henry said to Alan.

4. Zoe explained to her breakdown service that her car had broken down and she needed a mechanic.

My car has broken down and I need a mechanic, Zoe explained to her breakdown service.

5. *I scored 100% in the maths test,* Will told his parents as soon as he got home.

As soon as he got home, Will told his parents that he had scored 100% in the maths test.

Episode Twelve

Difficult Conversations

This section develops the story and revises and develops reported speech.

....

Good morning all! Pietro declared with unusual friendliness as he sat down at the table. He had already served himself from the buffet and had decided to pile two plates full of food, one with bacon, eggs and sausages from the Full English section and the other with croissants and other pastries from the Continental Buffet.

You didn't ask for that last night Pietro, his Mum whispered and she turned slightly red with embarrassment. Like her husband, Mrs Pasquati believed in honesty and was aware of the price difference between the two breakfasts.

I wasn't hungry last night and I am now, Pietro replied angrily. *Can you stop criticising me! It's only a small difference.*

Yes, and those regular small differences that Mrs Luca made every week resulted in a very large difference. It cost my company a lot and …. Mr Pasquati stopped. He had set his mobile at full volume to be sure of hearing the alarm and the music from his call was embarrassingly high. *It's Jamie,* he explained to his wife. *This could be difficulty. I'd told him we planned to be at his place by mid-afternoon today. I did try to call him last night, but there was no reply. The signal here is poor, so I'll take this call somewhere else.* Mr Pasquati took a quick sip of coffee, rose to his feet and strode off while fiddling (1) with his mobile.

Who's Jamie, Mum? Pietro immediately demanded.

Jamie is Mr MacDonald. You seem to have forgotten that we are going to stay with him and his family for a couple of weeks, his mother replied. Mrs Pasquati was trying to control her irritation.

Ah well. That's something I want to talk to you about, Pietro explained slowly. *Last night Michele asked me to go to Sicily for ten days with him and some mates. I've really gone off this Scotland idea. Can I go back home? It would make your holiday so much nicer not to have me around…I know I sometimes get on your nerves (2). It's age you know.*

Mrs Pasquati laughed. *My age or your age? I have some questions for you. One, do you have your key to the flat? Two, how much money do you have?*

Err, Pietro hesitated. *No. I don't have my key. And I have about 50 pounds and 200 euros in cash and another 400 in my account at home. The one you pay money into for university.*

His mother smiled in a way which Pietro knew meant trouble. *Good. No key, so that means you cannot get into the flat and wreck it. Your Dad spent about 130 euros each way for your flight, so if you give us the 50 pounds and your 200 euros that will pay for the wasted flights. That leaves you with the money in your uni (3) account to pay for your flight back today and for your holiday with Michele. You will need to stay with him when you come back from Sicily because we'll be in Scotland. You will not (4) get any more money until the new semester starts. If that suits you, you can go and find a flight.*

I hate parents so much, Pietro mumbled *(5)*. He was about to get up when he realised that the lady who had been working at the restaurant's door was looking at him. She had been collecting some of the used dishes from their table.

I'm sure it was a simple mistake, she said with a big smile, *but I think you only paid for the Continental and you are clearly enjoying a very large Full English. I'm sure it's your first time here, but please remember in future that there is a difference in price. Have a good day,* and she walked away with her hands full of plates.

A problem? Mr Pasquati had returned and noticed the look on his wife's face.

Yes, but I'll tell you later. And how was the conversation with Jamie?

Not very good. But I'll tell you about that later too. For now, can we go and check out and I'll tell you on the way to the car hire. Time to make a move, he said turning to Francesca and Pietro.

But I haven't finished my breakfast yet, Pietro complained, looking at the food still piled on one of his plates.

Then you need to learn to get up on time, his mother snapped *(6)*. *Are you coming with us or going back to Michele?*

Vocabulary and Culture

1. *fiddling To fiddle* with something means to touch and perhaps try to change an object. The suggestion here may be that Mr Pasquati is not very good at using his mobile.

To fiddle also has a widely used meaning of doing something wrong or unlawful.

Some examples: The teacher **fiddled the examination marks** to make sure that all his students passed the exam.

Mrs Luca **fiddled the money** from Mr Pasquati's company and that caused the company to make a loss.

2. *I know I sometime get on your nerves.* To get on someone's nerves is to upset someone, to make someone angry, to annoy someone.

Some examples:

My husband always spends the evening looking at his mobile, even when he says that we are watching a programme together. **It really gets on my nerves.**

When I was young I **used to get on my little sister's nerves** by hiding her favourite doll.

The wall in the hotel was so thin that we could hear everything the couple next door were saying. After two days it started **to get on our nerves** and we asked to change rooms.

3. *uni.* The short form for university. This is often used.

4. *You will not get any more money.* Here, Mrs Pasquati is using the longer, more formal *You will not get* rather than *You'll not get* for emphasis to make it clear to Pietro that no extra money will be given to him.

In speech there would be a lot of emphasis on *will* and *not.* She could also have said *You* **won't** *get any more money,* but this is also weaker than the original.

5. *mumbled.* To mumble means to say something in an unclear way. Probably with a low voice. The intention may be that the other person(s) will not hear what you are saying.

6. *snapped.* In this context, to say something quickly and with anger or aggression.

Some examples:

Can you stop snapping at me *every time I say something. You are in a very bad mood today,* Mark said to his girlfriend.

I was watching that programme. Change back to my channel immediately! You are really rude! Victoria **snapped at** her teenage son.

Comprehension

1. Why was Mrs Pasquati embarrassed?

2. What had Mrs Luca been doing in Mr Pasquati's company?

3. What was the problem with the volume on Mr Pasquati's mobile?

4. Which verb tells you that Mr Pasquati moved quite quickly? What is the infinitive of this verb?

5. Which verb indicates that Mr Pasquati <u>might not</u> have a good understanding of his mobile?

6. What were the 4 reasons Pietro gave for wanting to join Michele and his mates in Sicily?

7. What was Mrs Pasquati's concern about Pietro (and his mates?)?

Questions 8 and 9 are tricky. A reminder that when you take some exams, or tests, you may be asked for *True, False or Not Given.*

<u>It is therefore important to look at both the question and information carefully.</u>

8. How much had Mr Pasquati paid for the family's flights to London?

9. Did Mr Pasquati eat all his porridge?

Something to consider

What do you normally have for breakfast when you are at home? Could you describe it in English? When do you have breakfast? Is your breakfast healthy or unhealthy? What reasons do you give for your answer?

Answers

Comprehension

1. Mrs Pasquati was embarrassed because Pietro had ordered the Continental Breakfast but taken food from the Full English. There was a difference in price between the two and Mrs Pasquati believed in honesty.

2. Mrs Luca had been fiddling money from Mr Pasquati's company. We don't know how much and how, but she had cost Mr Pasquati's company *a lot*.

3. The volume on Mr Pasquati's mobile had been set to a high level to wake him up. The volume was embarrassing in the restaurant.

4. *Strode,* which means to walk with long steps and implies speed and purpose. The infinitive is *to stride*

5. Mr Pasquati was fiddling with his phone. When applied to technology, to fiddle may imply adjusting something carefully, or to try to work something without fully understanding how it works (in most cases it is the second use).

6. Pietro said that he had gone off the idea of going to Scotland and that it was better for his parents not to have him around because he sometime got on their nerves. He explained that it was because of his age.

7. Mrs Pasquati was worried that Pietro and his mates might <u>wreck (destroy or damage)</u> the family's flat.

Questions 8 and 9 are tricky. A reminder that when you take some exams, or tests, you may be asked for *True, False or Not Given.*

It is therefore important to look at both the question and information carefully.

8. We know that *Your Dad spent about 130 euros <u>each way</u> for your flight.*

There were 4 people in the group so the flight to London had cost 130x4 = 520 euros

Answer: Mr Pasquati had paid 520 euros for the **family's** flights **to London**?

9. We do not know the answer to this. Mr Pasquati ordered some porridge when he arrived, but there is no evidence that it was ready before he left.

We do not know if he had an opportunity to eat the porridge

Episode Thirteen

The Car Rental

Checking out? The speaker was a young man who, Mr Pasquati decided, was probably Polish to judge from the accent.

Yes. Rooms 232 and 467. Where do I leave the keys?

Everything was OK? The man enquired and looked down at the computer console to confirm the rooms. *Mr Pasquati? Just drop the keys in the box. Have a good day. We hope to see you again soon.*

Thanks. OK. Everyone ready? Mr Pasquati asked, turning to his family. *Ah Pietro, your Mum tells me you are going to Sicily and not Scotland for your holiday. Is that right? They both begin with S – did you get confused?*

Pietro laughed. *At least they both begin with S. Doesn't Stansted have an S and Gatwick a G? At least I haven't got the wrong airport. But no. I have decided to stay with you and enjoy my holiday looking after you. I don't want you to get lost on the way north.*

Stop being so cheeky Pietro! His mother spoke so loudly that both staff at the reception desk raised their heads. *Can we stop bickering (1) and go and get our car? What did Jamie say Enrico?* Mrs Pasquati asked her husband as they started to wheel their cases towards the hotel's exit.

He was not very pleased, her husband replied slowly. *It seems… No. Let me tell you in the car. We really need to start moving north.*

Enrico. Why didn't we just fly to Edinburgh or Glasgow instead of London? Mrs Pasquati whispered as soon as Pietro and Francesca were out of earshot.

There were very few direct flights from Bologna and we would have lost a day going to Milano. And it was much more expensive, Enrico replied immediately. *Come on. They are leaving us behind.*

Twenty minutes later the family arrived at the car hire company's counter. Pietro had looked online, seen the cost of a return flight to Italy and tried again to persuade his parents to lend him the money. He had failed, and had immediately decided that going to Scotland, and staying with the MacDonalds, would not be so bad after all.

Good morning. My name is Pasquti. I spoke to Emily last night and she said that she would arrange (2) a car for us for this morning.

Good morning sir. Yes, Emily explained the situation when she finished her shift this morning. The speaker was a smartly-dressed man in his forties, some grey starting to appear in his beard and a red Sikh turban sitting on his head. *Do you want the good news or the bad?* And he smiled.

Mrs Pasquati giggled. *Only the good please. Yesterday was bad enough.*

Well, the bad news is that we cannot get the model you booked from Stansted, or one of our local depots, until this afternoon. The good news is that I can offer you a superior vehicle for the same price – I see from the company's records that Mr Pasquati is a regular customer. There is no extra charge, not even for the insurance. But, I must warn you that this model is a bit heavier on fuel, even though it's a diesel, and it's also quite a large vehicle. Are you OK with that?

And that's available now? Mr Pasquati said with relief in his voice. *If so, yes. Thank you for being so helpful*

Our pleasure. And yes, it's already been serviced and valeted so if you are happy all I need is your credit card as a deposit, sight of you driving licence and for you to sign the hire and insurance documents. You asked for your wife to be the second driver so I need to see her licence too.

Mrs. Pasquati unzipped her handbag, took out her purse, opened it and then her face paled. *Enrico. I…I don't have it. I'm so sorry Enrico. It was in my other purse. I forgot to put it in my handbag.*

So I have to do all the driving? Mr Pasquati could not hide his irritation. *That was not what we agreed.*

Don't worry Dad. I have my licence! Pietro announced with pleasure and he waved his new licence in his father's face. For Pietro, access to a car meant that he would have greater freedom during the holiday.

Great! That would be helpful. I'd like to add my son instead of my wife Mr Singh, he said. The man had just pinned a badge inscribed *G. Singh, Location Manager* to his jacket.

Mr Singh hesitated. *How old is your son, sir?*

I'm twenty, twenty one in a month, Pietro replied proudly.

Mr Pasquati, I'm afraid that if you take the vehicle I offered you it will cost you an arm and a leg for the insurance (3). Under 25s pay a huge premium on the insurance and a very substantial excess.*

How much extra? Mr Pasquati enquired slowly, and it was his turn to pale when Mr Singh told him the price. *Do you have anything smaller and cheaper that my son can drive?*

Twenty minutes later they had managed to squeeze (3) their cases into a smaller car. This, Mr Singh had said, was a good size vehicle for the small roads in Scotland. The family was sitting in the car and Mr Pasquati was adjusting his seat when his mobile rang. He answered, listened to the caller and then put his face in his hands. *That was the hotel. Francesca, you left your jacket in the room. Please run and get it from reception. Be quick please. One day we may actually start this holiday.*

Vocabulary and Culture

(1) To bicker: to argue in an unfriendly manner, probably over a long period of time. Children in a family often bicker over what adults may think are unimportant things.

(2) I spoke to Emily last night and she said that she would arrange a car for us this morning.

Notice carefully what happens to *I will* in reported speech in sentences like this. Emily actually said: *I **will arrange** a car for you for tomorrow morning.*

(3) …it will cost you an arm and a leg for the insurance. To cost an arm and a leg means to be very expensive.

It can sometime, rarely, be used to describe the cost of a decision. For example: *I really do not approve of your choice of husband. If you insist on marrying him it will cost you an arm and a leg because I'll exclude you from my will!* The girl's old aunt shouted.

A Cultural Note

Under 25s pay a huge premium on the insurance and a very substantial excess.*

In Britain the insurance on a car is based on 1. The model, age and value of the vehicle, 2. The age and driving experience of the drivers and 3. The number of traffic offences.

If you are under 25 you normally pay *a premium* (more money) because data shows that this age group has more accidents.

The *excess* is the amount you have to pay before the insurance company starts to pay for damage. Typically, this is around £200 but could increase to £1,000 or more if your licence indicates that you are a bad driver.

Comprehension

Ensure you use the correct tenses

1. In what way, and why, was Pietro bickering with his father?

2. Why did the staff at the hotel look at the family?

3. What evidence is there <u>in this section</u> that Pietro did not want to continue this holiday with his parents?

4. What did Pietro do between the hotel and the car hire* company? *[* Note that car hire and car rental are essentially inter-changeable.]*

5. Why was Mrs Pasquati upset and Pietro pleased?

6. What was the consequence of this difference between mother and son?

7. What type of suitcases did the family have?

8. Which physical reaction showed that Mr and Mrs Pasquati were both shocked?

9. Why did Francesca have to return to the hotel? Where did she have to go?

Something Different

Can you remember how to give and follow directions in English?

Do you remember the basics such as?

Turn right / left.

Turn 1st / 2nd / 3rd left

Go straight on.

It's on your right / left.

You'll see it straight in front of you / on your left/on your right.

It will* be facing you on your left/on your right.

It will* be just behind you.

If you arrive at XXXXX you have gone too far.

If you turn to your right/left

If you look to your right/left

You need to turn around / to your right / left.

You need to turn slightly right/left

You need to turn sharp right / left

Follow the road / path / walkway until you arrive at

*It'll is used in speech and informal text.

Below, is a map of Gatwick North Terminal's ground floor level.

The Pasquatis have walked past the Security Office on the first floor and taken the escalator down to the ground floor. They have arrived with *Coral* slightly to their right.

Mrs Pasquati wanted to go to the ladies and she asks you how to get there.

Mr Pasquati asks you how to get to the car rental.

What are your directions?

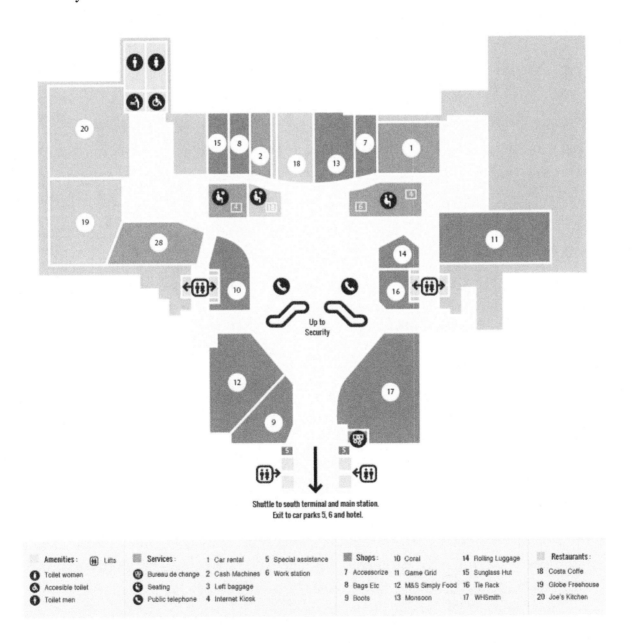

Answers

1. Pietro had decided that he wanted to return home so that he could go on holiday with his friend Michele.

Because his parents had refused to help him, he made fun of the fact that his father had booked a flight to the wrong airport. This was partly in revenge for his father's comment *Mum tells me you are going to Sicily and not Scotland for your holiday. Is that right? They both begin with S – did you get confused?*

Pietro retaliated with *At least they both begin with S. Doesn't Stansted have an S and Gatwick a G? At least I haven't got the wrong airport.*

And then insulted his father by saying *I don't want you to get lost on the way north.*

Both Mr Pasquati and Pietro are being sarcastic. Who do you think wins this verbal battle? Why? Can you explain your answer in English?

2. The staff at the hotel look at them because Mrs Pasquati raised her voice because she was angry with Pietro. *Stop being so cheeky Pietro!*

3. Pietro is rude to his father [*Do you agree?*] by making fun of him. He also tried to persuade his parents to lend him the money to go back to Italy. [*Note: he had done this before, but you do not need to mention this because the question is concerned only with* this section.]

4. Pietro checked the prices for flights once again and when his parents refused to lend him the money he decided that he had no choice but to go to Scotland. [*He resigned himself to going to Scotland*].

5. Mrs Pasquati was upset because she **had left** [Note the use of the past perfect] her driving licence in a purse in Italy and Pietro was pleased because he **had brought** his driving licence and thought he would have more freedom by using the hire car.

6. Initially Mr Pasquati was upset because he and his wife **had agreed** to share the driving. Mrs Pasquatio was upset and embarrassed and Pietro was pleased because he wanted the freedom of being able to drive the car.

7. The Pasquatis *wheeled their cases towards the hotel's exit* so they had wheeled cases. I think you can also answer that their suitcases were not small. Why? A). They were going to Scotland for two weeks. B. They needed a large vehicle and when they got a smaller vehicle they had *to squeeze* their cases into the car.

8. Mr and Mrs Pasquati both **paled** when they were shocked. Mrs Pasquati was upset because **she'd** forgotten her driving licence and Mr Pasquati was shocked when he heard the difference in price between the two cars.

9. Francesca had to return to the hotel because **she'd** forgotten her jacket. She had to go to the hotel reception.

Instructions

There are a number of possibilities, but these are the easiest and clearest.

Mrs Pasquati: *If you look to your right, you will see the seating area for Costa Coffee and the restaurant behind it. Walk towards Costa's* and when you come to the end of Coral turn slightly left. You will see the Globe Freehouse in front of you. Walk towards it and then take a sharp right. You will see the toilets directly in front of you.*

Mr Pasquati: *If you look to your right, you will see the seating area for Costa Coffee and the restaurant behind it. Walk towards Costa's and when you see a Work station area on your right, turn slightly right and walk past Monsoon and Accessorize which are on your left. You will find the car rental on your left, facing the Internet kiosk.*

[**Cultural note.** Many people still write and pronounce shops names using the possessive. This dates from the time when the shop was owned by a person or an identified company. So you will hear people refer to Smith's, Tesco's, Sainsbury's etc.*
This is not often used when talking about stores which are newer on the market and the use of the possessive' is disappearing on store names and among younger people. It will sound strange though if you say you are shopping at Tesco and not at Tesco's.]

Episode Fourteen

Mr MacDonald*

This section focuses on the use of reported speech and the past perfect.

It also contains some cultural information.

Francesca immediately got out of the car and darted (1) back the way the family had just come. Not only did she love her jacket, an expensive present from the previous Xmas(2), but she had left almost all her holiday money in a purse in one of the zipped inside pockets.

So Enrico, what did Jamie say? Mrs Pasquati immediately asked. She was anxious to hear what had been said.

He was not pleased, her husband immediately replied. *They had arranged a surprise trip for us to visit a place called the Orkneys +.*

Orkneys? What's that? Pietro asked. He had been sitting in the back of the car and, unusually, was listening to his parents and not playing a game on his mobile.

Jamie said that they are islands north of Inverness. Margaret wanted to see them because she has an interest in archaeology and he said that this place is very important for that. And apparently there is an interesting Italian church there.

*An Italian church? ^*Mrs Pasquati asked with surprise. *So far north? Strange. But can't we go later?*

Perhaps, but it was meant to be part of an anniversary surprise for Margaret, their 24th anniversary, and he'd booked a really nice hotel for both families.

Oh dear. We are not going to be popular. But he can cancel the hotel? Mrs Pasquati asked anxiously. She liked the MacDonalds and did not want to upset them.

Perhaps not. It was another of these fixed price deals the British use so much. He is going to try, but he has his doubts.

So should we go home then? Pietro asked hopefully. *No point going to visit if we are unpopular.*

Mr Pasquati turned in his seat so that he could look his son in the face. *I am getting sick and tired (3) of your comments Pietro. You had the chance to go back and didn't take it. So stop whining(4) and make the best of this holiday. Ah. Good. Here is Francesca. Did you get your jacket OK?* He asked as Francesca opened the door and got into the car.

Yes, and all my money. They'd put it in the safe and made me check it was the right amount before I left. They were nice. Very helpful.

And especially the Polish lad I bet (5), Pietro immediately taunted (6). *I could see you quite fancied him (7).*

Vocabulary and Culture

*Mac as in Macdonald or sometime Mc as in McDonalds both have their roots in Scottish or Irish and both mean *son of*. So McPherson means *son of the parson* (priest) in old Scottish.

+The Orkneys are a group of islands just off the coast of north east Scotland.

Because of their shape, they are often described as looking like whales in the sea.

The islands were part of Norway until 1468 when they became part of Scotland.

^ The Italian church in the Orkneys was built by Italian prisoners of war during the Second World War.

(1) To Dart is *to move quickly*. It is usually used for people and animals in sentences such as:

The cat **darted** *across the garden when it tried to catch the bird.*

The lady **darted** *across the road when she saw her bus turn the corner.*

The origins are related to this type of weapon and hunting tool

though in Europe you are more likely to know it in this form as darts in the dartboard. This was a good score!

(2) Xmas is inter-changeable with **Christmas.**

(3) *sick and tired of…* This is a fixed term so you need both parts. <u>It is quite a strong term to use.</u> The meaning is *bored by, made angry by, frustrated by* as in:

When Martha told her mother that she was **sick and tired of** *her cooking, her mother told her to cook for the rest of the week.*

Helen was **sick and tired of** *her boyfriend always going out with other girls he fancied, so she left him.*

After 40 minutes Will was **sick and tired of** *waiting for the food which he had ordered, so he cancelled his order and walked out of the restaurant.*

(4) *whining* **To whine** is to constantly, or very frequently, complain about something or to criticise. It is linked to the sound that machinery can make when it produces a constant noise. Or sometimes with animals as in the sound an unhappy dog can make.

Jack told his worker to stop **whining** *or to start looking for a new job.*

The **whine** *of the engines increased as the aircraft increased its speed.*

The puppy did not stop **whining** *until its mother fed her.*

Comprehension

1. How did Francesca move from the car back to the hotel?

2. Why was Francesca anxious about her jacket?

3. What had the hotel done with her money? Why?

4. Why did Mrs Pasquati want to immediately know about the conversation with Mr MacDonald?

5. What is the name of Mr MacDonald's wife? [Use a complete sentence in your answer, not one word].

6. What was special about this time?

7. In what way was Pietro's behaviour unusual for him?

8. Francesca was pleased with the hotel but had reason to be upset or angry with Pietro. Why was this?

Answers to the Comprehension

1. Francesca darted back to the hotel from the car.

2. Francesca was anxious about her jacket because it had been a Xmas present and because her purse in one of the pockets contained her holiday money.

3. The hotel staff had put Francesca money in a safe. Why? To keep it safe.

4 Mrs Pasquati liked the MacDonalds and did not want to upset them.

5. The name of Mr MacDonald's wife was Margaret.

6. The MacDonald's 24th wedding anniversary was about this time and Mr MacDonald had planned the trip to the Orkneys because his wife was interested in archaeology.

7. Pietro was actually listening to his parents rather than playing games on his mobile.

8. The hotel had contacted her about her jacket and had looked after it and her money safely. They had even counted the money with her.

She had reason to be upset with her brother because he taunted her about the young Polish man at reception and the possibility that Francesca *fancied him.*

Reported speech

Before we start, here is some grammar revision.

You will almost certainly already know and understand the First Conditional (it has other names but that is not important).

If it has other names, (the condition) *it is not important* (the result).

If I read something in the Future Conditional, (the condition) *I will understand it* (the result).

In reported speech, **If** is used regularly to communicate both conditional ideas and mental and physical staes.

So, *Are you happy?* Becomes *S/he asked me* **if I was happy.**

Are you comfortable? Becomes *S/he asked me* **if I was comfortable.**

Do you like large or small cars? Becomes *S/he asked me* **if I liked large or small cars.**

Cultural Note

*It is becoming more common when writing to use **s/he** as a structure when the gender is unclear.

Historically, **he** was used, but this is now increasingly regarded as sexist.

For example, **some** departments (mostly in literature and the social sciences to the best of my knowledge) in some universities now penalise gender specific structure.

In any language, you need to adjust your style according to your audience.

If is also used **to communicate uncertainty:**

Can you tell me if this train goes to London or Birmingham? The lady asked.

The lady asked if the train went to London or Birmingham.

If you turn right at the end of the road, *you will see the shop directly in front of you,* the policeman explained.

The policeman explained that, **if we turned right at the end of the road,** we would see the shop directly in front of us.

If you lend me £10 now, *I'll give you £11 next week,* the girl explained to Mary.

The girl explained to her friend that, **if she lent her £10 then,** she would receive £11 the following week.

[+ It is also possible to say I <u>shall</u> understand it or <u>we shall understand it</u> . Don't worry, we shall return to this issue, so **stay with will for now.]**

Let us look at some parts of the original story. [Note the use of **If**]

1. Checking out? The speaker was a young man who, Mr Pasquati decided, was probably Polish to judge from the accent.

In reported speech this would be:

The young man asked if the family was checking out.

Notice the use of *if* here to communicate uncertainty.

2. Yes. Rooms 232 and 467. Where do I leave the keys?

In reported speech this would be:

Mr Pasquati confirmed that he was checking out, said that the family had stayed in rooms 232 and 467, and asked where he <u>should</u> leave the keys.

Notice the use of <u>should</u> here to communicate uncertainty and to ask for clarification

3. Everything was OK? The man enquired and looked down at the computer console to confirm the rooms. *Mr Pasquati? Just drop the keys in the box. Have a good day. We hope to see you again soon.*

In reported speech this would be:

The man asked if everything had been ok, checked the room numbers and name, wished Mr Pasquati a good day and said that he hoped that they would return to the hotel.

4. Good morning. My name is Pasquti. I spoke to Emily last night and she said that she would arrange a car for us for this morning.

In reported speech this would be:

Mr Pasquati wished the person at the desk a good morning and explained that he had spoken to Emily the previous night [you could also say 'last night' in this situation] and she had said that she would arrange a car for the family that morning.

Notice how that past perfect is used here and how *this morning* becomes *that morning.*

Why? Because in reported speech time may have changed, so it may no longer be *this morning.*

5. Good morning sir. Yes, Emily explained the situation when she finished her shift this morning. The speaker was a smartly-dressed man in his forties, some grey starting to appear in his beard and a dark red Sikh turban sitting on his head. *Do you want the good news or the bad?* And he smiled.

<u>In reported speech this would be</u>:

The man wished Mr Pasquati a good morning and told him that Emily had explained the situation when she had finished the shift that morning. He asked Mr Pasquati if he wanted to hear the good, or the bad, news.

Some Sentences for you to try. [These are perhaps a bit easier].

Try turning these sentences into reported speech. <u>Look carefully at the small changes and punctuation, and think about changes in tense.</u>

<u>Try this before you look at the answers below.</u>

1. *I like holidays,* Emma said.

2. *My name is Julia,* the woman said.

3. *I like holidays!* Emma declared.

4. *In English, Wednesday comes from the Scandinavian name for the god Woden,* the teacher explained to the class.

5. *When I grow up I want to work in a bank and be very rich,* the little boy explained.

6. *Are you feeling any better?* The nurse asked the patient.

7. *We went to Morocco for a holiday last year, but we didn't see very much because the weather was terrible,* James explained to his parents.

8. *If you are all sitting quietly children, I'll start the story,* the teacher said.

9. *If you all stop talking, I'll start the story,* the teacher explained.

10. The islands were part of Norway until 1468 when they became part of Scotland.

 [This is not spoken but the same rules apply to written work]

<u>The Answers are:</u>

1. Emma said that she liked holidays.

2. The woman said that her name was Julia

3. Emma declared that she liked holidays

4. The teacher explained to the class that, in English, the word Wednesday came from the Scandinavian name for the god Woden.

5. The little boy explained that he wanted to work in a bank and be very rich when he grew up.

6. The nurse asked the patient if s/he* was feeling better. [It is also possible to say: *The nurse asked the patient if they were feeling better.* This is a common structure and avoids she / he decisions]

7. James explained to his parents that they had gone to Morocco the previous year but they hadn't enjoyed it very much because the weather was terrible.

8. The teacher told the children that s/ he would start the story if they were sitting comfortable.

9. The teacher told the children that s/he would start the story if they all sat quietly

10. The paragraph said that the islands had been part of Norway until 1468 when they became part of Scotland.

[Yes, the page did not speak but the word *said* is still widely used. An example: The newspaper article **said** that the government planned to spend more money on education.]

Episode Fifteen

Yet Another Change

Mr Pasquati felt a surge (1) of relief as he finally turned the ignition key, backed out of the parking bay, shifted the car into first gear and started to drive towards the exit. It was a short lived journey (2).

Wrong side of the road Dad! Francesca shouted. Mr Pasquati swerved across into the correct lane and almost ran over Mr Singh who had darted out of the office door. He signalled Mr Pasquati to stop.

Oh no. Another problem, Mrs Pasquati sighed.

I can't believe this, Mr Pasquati mumbled as Mr Singh tapped on the side window. *How can I help you Mr Singh?*

Perhaps I can help you sir, the car rental manager said with a broad smile, though he had paled slightly because of the near accident. *I hope I have good news for you. It's rather unusual but…*and he paused. *We have a client at Stansted Airport who doesn't want to take the car we had reserved for you because it's too big for her. That was the only car we have. She hadn't reserved, which was very unwise for this time of year. But, like you, she is a very good customer.*

So? Mr Pasquati enquired.

Well sir, you have a car here which, if I am totally honest, is a little too small for you and your family and your long journey to Scotland. The regional manager has suggested that you can have the original car if you are prepared to go to Stansted airport, drop this car and collect your original. The one you had reserved originally.

Stansted is almost on our route isn't it? Mr Pasquati enquired.

Yes, if you take the M11 onto the A1 you pass the airport. And, because of the fact that you are a regular customer and you are helping us and the other client, the regional manager has told me I can remove the excesses and surplus for your son.

Really?

Yes sir. We do not normally do this, but we are making an exception to help two of our regulars.

Great! Pietro shouted from the back seat. *I can drive a big car!*

Ten minutes later the Pasquatis were driving north along the M23 (3) towards the junction with the M25. There was very little traffic and Mr Singh had told them to take the M25 and then the M11. Mr Pasquati had always driven straight into the centre of London from Gatwick. However, Pietro had insisted on programming their car's sat nav which he said would ensure they got to Stansted without any problems.

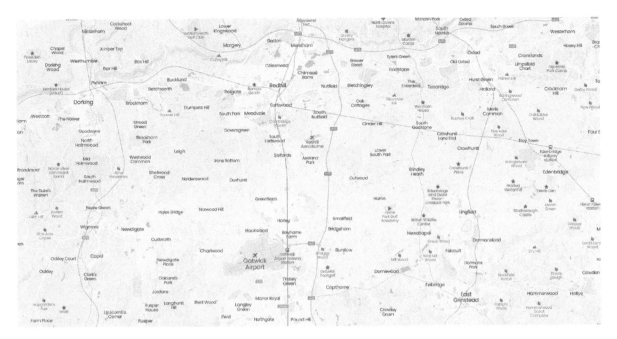

The M23 is the orange road running north-south.

The M25 is the orange road running east-west.

Finally! We are making progress, Mrs Pasquati said happily. *When do you think we'll arrive in Inverness Enrico?*

Ah. There's a problem, Mr Pasquati replied slowly. *Jamie rang this morning while you were in the shower and explained that the ferry company is prepared to refund their passage but the hotel is not. So either they go or they lose hundreds of pounds and Margaret is going to be very upset. So, they are going to go to the Orkneys and that means we have to delay our arrival.*

Really? That isn't very nice.

Mr Pasquati shook his head slowly. *It's our fault. My fault. They arranged everything around our arrival. We should already be there and the ferry and hotels were booked for tonight.*

So we can arrive tomorrow? Francesca asked.

No. They are away for 3 nights, so we have to organise something between now and then. Francesca, you are the great explorer. Can you look at the old map you brought with you and suggest some places we can visit between here and Inverness.

Vocabulary and Culture

(1) *a surge of relief.* A surge is a sudden, strong **feeling** or **movement.**

Some examples:

The waves **surged up** the beach and almost knocked Louise off her feet.

After the Roman troops had made a hole in the city's wall **they surged forward** into the city.

The car **surged forward** as soon as Peter put it into gear and it almost crashed into the car in front.

Robert felt **a surge of sadness** when he went back to see the house he had lived in as a child.

Helen experienced **a surge of anger** when she saw the mess her children had made while she was out at the shops.

As soon as it got dark Peter felt **a sudden surge of fear.** He was totally lost and could hear the wolves crying in the distance.

There was **a surge in viewing numbers** when a famous actor appeared on the Saturday evening television show.

(2). *It was short lived.* As the name suggests, something which is short lived does not last for long.

Some examples:

Bruce fell madly in love with Abigail, but she didn't really feel the same and the **romance was short lived**. After three months they had already split up.

Our neighbours have some interesting plants in their front garden, but some of them have **flowers which are very short lived** and the flowers are dead within a week.

Maggie enjoyed working and living in Boston, but her stay there was **quite short lived.** After only six months her company moved her to New York.

The Big Boot's **run on Amazon was short lived**. After only four episodes Amazon pulled it from their server.

M is the standard short form for Motorway and on British maps are usually marked in blue.

A class roads are important routes and are usually marked in red.

B class roads are often less important and are usually marked in orange.

White (sometimes called C class) roads are minor roads which **may** be very narrow and slow.

Comprehension and an Exercise

You need to ensure that you use the correct tense and reported speech structure to answer these questions correctly. There is a reminder of some useful grammar below this comprehension section and you may wish to look at that.

1. How did Mr Pasquati feel when he started the hire car?

2. In which direction did Mr Pasquati first drive?

3. Looking at the evidence from this story, why is it perhaps surprising that Francesca shouted *Wrong side of the road Dad!?*

4. What evidence is there to show that Mr Singh left his office in a hurry?

5. Why did Mr Singh look pale?

6. What was the first thing Mr Pasquati asked Mr Singh?

7. What could have happened if Mr Pasquati had not stopped the car and spoken to Mr Singh?

7. Who had Mr Singh spoken to before stopping the Pasquati's car?

8. When Mr Pasquati returns to Italy, he tells one of his friends about the conversation with Mr Singh. Using the correct forms of reported speech, turn the conversation below into an accurate report of what happened.

Start with:

We were just driving away when the manager from the rental company darted out of his office. I almost hit him with the car, but then he tapped on the car window and said…………..

I hope I have good news for you. It's rather unusual but… and he paused. *We have a client at Stansted Airport who doesn't want to take the car we had reserved for you because it's too big for her. That was the only car we have. She hadn't reserved, which was very unwise for this time of year. But, like you, she is a very good customer.*

So? Mr Pasquati enquired.

Well sir, you have a car here which, if I am totally honest, is a little too small for you and your family and your long journey to Scotland. The regional manager has suggested that you can have the original car if you are prepared to go to Stansted airport, drop this car and collect your original. The one you had reserved originally.

A Reminder of Some Grammar

The past perfect and its use with the Historical Conditional (it has other names but that is not important) is a very useful, and important, structure to understand and use but it is often neglected.

For example:

Alfred fell because Henry hit him tells us very little, but *Alfred fell because Henry had hit him* tells us much more and seems to suggest that it was Henry who had started the fight.

So, we can extend this: *Alfred hit Henry because Henry had hit Alfred. The fight would not have started if Alfred had not insulted Henry's girlfriend.*

Notice the use of the present perfect, past perfect and *if*.

The present perfect is associated with the condition *The fight would not have started if*

The past perfect is associated with <u>the result</u> *Alfred had not insulted Henry's girlfriend.*

The position of *if* may be at the start of the sentence: *If Alfred had not insulted Henry's girlfriend, the fight would not have started* or in the middle of the sentence as above.

<u>Note that there is usually a comma if the sentence starts with *if*.</u>

Let us look at these sentences:

1. The MacDonalds left Inverness without waiting for the Pasquatis.

The Pasquatis arrived at the wrong airport and were late.

The combined conditional sequences could be:

If the Pasquatis had not arrived at the wrong airport, they would not have been late and the MacDonalds would not have left Inverness without them.

2. Mr Singh had darted out of the office door. He signalled Mr Pasquati to stop.

The combined conditional sequences could be:

If Mr Singh had been slower, Mr Pasquati would have passed the office and they would not have had a conversation.

Look out for similar structures.

<u>Answers to the Comprehension and an Exercise</u>

1. Mr Pasquati felt a surge of relief when he started the car. *(as he finally turned the ignition key)*

2. Mr Pasquati first drove backwards. (He *backed out of the parking bay*)

3. There is no evidence from the story that Francesca knew how to drive. Both Mrs Pasquati and Pietro had driving licences and therefore had some experience of driving.

Both were older than Francesca, so they had more responsibility.

Francesca was also in the back of the car, while Mrs Pasquati was in the front next to her husband.

It is therefore a little surprising that she realised that her father was doing something wrong.

4. Mr Singh *darted* out of his office.

5. Mr Pasquati looked pale because Mr Pasquati had swerved the car and had almost hit him [so Mr Singh was shocked – **you do not have to add this**].

6. Mr Pasquati asked Mr Singh if he could help him.

7. If Mr Pasquati had not stopped the car, Mr Singh would not have told him about the possibility of exchanging cars at Stansted airport. So the family could have driven to Scotland in a smaller and less comfortable car than they wanted.

7. Mr Singh had spoken to his regional manager.

8. When Mr Pasquati returns to Italy, he tells one of his friends about the conversation with Mr Singh. Using the correct forms of reported speech, turn the conversation below into an accurate report of what happened.

Start with:

We were just driving away when the manager from the rental company darted out of his office. I almost hit him with the car, but then he tapped on the car window and said that he had good news for me. He told me [or explained or said] that his suggestion was rather unusual but his company had a client at Stansted airport who didn't want to take the car that we had reserved because it was too big for her, but that was the only car available. He thought that she had been unwise because she hadn't booked a car, but that this person [or lady] was a good customer like me.

When I asked him why he was telling me this he said [or explained or told me] that he thought our car was too small for the family for the long trip to Scotland and the regional manager had suggested that we drive to Stansted and swap cars so we could have the car we had originally reserved.

Episode Sixteen

Stansted Airport

We were lucky, Mrs Pasquati commented   as they turned off the M25 and onto the M11 which was signposted for **Stansted Airport and Cambridge.** *Did you see that tail back* (1) *on the other side of the motorway? It must have been at least ten miles long.*

Where are we Mum? Francesca asked, sitting upright in her seat and looking outside the car. Both she and Pietro had fallen asleep soon after leaving Gatwick but only after they had argued because she said that Pietro was taking up too much space with all his *useless stuff* as she called his laptop, mobile phone and the latest device for playing his music. This was so new that no one knew (2) what it was called apart from Pietro.

Just coming up to the airport, her Mum (3) replied. *We'll be there in a few minutes and then we can get going north. Did you manage to find some interesting places to visit on the way up? I saw you looking at your map and the Internet earlier. Did you have any luck?*

We have three days? Is that right? So we can do the journey in stages, Francesca replied enthusiastically. She hated long car journeys when there wasn't an opportunity to stop and explore, and had dreaded the idea of driving all the way from London to Inverness in one day. *I've seen Lincoln, York, Durham and Edinburgh as possible stops. It's just after ten now, so we can be in Lincoln this afternoon and explore it and perhaps stay there for the night. Do you want me to look for a hotel?*

Please. And ….. try to keep the cost down, Mrs Pasquati added. *We hadn't budgeted on these hotel stays on the way north. And can you turn off your brother's sat nav thing. We know where we are and where we are going, so we do not need that woman's voice every few minutes. It's so irritating.*

I'll do it. Leave my stuff alone Fran! Pietro hated people touching *my stuff* and his mother's instruction to Francesca had woken him. *Where are we? What's happening?* He demanded.

We're arriving, Mr Pasquati replied as he drove down the avenue next to the airport building. He turned sharp left into the car rental section and parked under a sign which read **Returned Vehicles.** Then he turned off the engine, undid his seat belt and opened the door. *Mum, can you and Francesca unload the car while I go and sort out the new vehicle. It's a lovely morning, so just wait here and enjoy the sun, and I'll come back in a few minutes. Pietro, I need you and your driving licence. Come on. Be quick. And please put your shoes on. You are not walking around with your socks and no shoes.*

Twenty minutes later they were on the M11 again. The change of vehicles had gone smoothly and the family was pleased to find that they had a much larger and more comfortable vehicle. So, have you found us a hotel for tonight Francesca? And where do you suggest we go now? Mr Pasquati enquired.

This Lincoln place looks interesting and we can get there quite quickly, Francesca replied immediately. She had already decided on a route and did not want Pietro to start making changes. *It's about 130 miles according to this web site (4) so about three and a half hours. And there is a Premier Inn there so we can get 3 rooms for £105 or go to the Hilton for £250.*

The Premier Inn will be fine unless you kids want to pay. Mr Pasquati replied. *Can you book for us online Fran?*

Why does it take so long? Pietro demanded. *I could do that in about an hour at home,* he declared proudly.

Really? Mrs Pasquati turned in her seat. *Are you confusing miles and kilometres or are you driving faster than your Dad and I would like? Anyway, what's there to see in this Lincoln place Fran?*

This extract about Lincoln is from Wikipedia and is what Francesca read to her parents. (The extract has been shortened and simplified)

The Lincoln bishops were among the richest people in medieval England. The estates (5) controlled by the bishop were the largest in England and contained more monasteries than the rest of England put together. When the nobles wrote the Magna Carta (6) in 1215, one of the witnesses was Hugh of Wells, Bishop of Lincoln. One of only four surviving originals of the document is in Lincoln Castle.

In 1141 Lincoln was the site of a battle between King Stephen, the grandson of William the Conqueror, and the army of Empress Matilda. After fierce fighting in the city's streets, Stephen's army was defeated and the king captured.

By 1150, Lincoln was among the wealthiest towns in England. The basis of the economy was cloth and wool which was exported to Flanders. Lincoln Cloth, especially the fine, dyed (7) scarlet and green were famous and the green became even more famous because it was connected with the outlaw Robin Hood who wore Lincoln Green.

Thirteenth-century Lincoln was England's third largest city and a favourite home of several kings. It was also home to one of the five main Jewish communities in England

Frontage of 12th century Jews' Court on Steep Hill.

During the First Barons' War, Lincoln was involved in the conflict between the king and rebel barons who had allied with the French. Here, and at Dover, the French and Rebel army was defeated. Lincoln was pillaged (8) because it had supported Prince Louis of France. In the Second Barons' War of 1266, the rebels attacked the Jews of Lincoln, and badly damaged their synagogue, because they had supported the king

A View of Lincoln Cathedral

Vocabulary and Culture

(1) **a tail back** is used as an alternative to **a queue** when talking about **traffic.** In American English it is also sometimes used to describe a queue of people.

(2) Notice the use of **new** and **knew** in the same sentence. They have totally different meanings, but the sounds could be confusing in an aural exam and you could lose marks by confusing the spelling in a written exam.

(3) **Mum** or mum? **Dad** or dad? The convention is that if you are talking about any mum or dad there is no capital, but your own Mum and Dad deserve a capital because they are important and The Bank of Mum and Dad is one of the most popular banks on the planet!

(4) **website.** As in point 2, remember the difference between **site** (e.g. a building site, the site of a battle, the site of my old school) and **sight** (e.g. my sight is not very good so I use glasses)

(5) **estates.** An estate is a <u>large</u> area of land which is usually used for farming or hunting. It is also used more generally to describe the possessions of a person who has died.

The first meaning has continued to describe a person who buys and sells houses. For example: *When we decided to sell our house, three* **estate agents** *came and gave us a <u>valuation</u>* (they stated what they thought was the value of the house and gardens).

The second meaning is clear in a sentence like this: *When Professor Morris died his estate was divided equally among his children. The estate included two houses, some valuable paintings, a new car and a very valuable collection of old stamps.*

(6) **Magna Carta.** Some people claim that Magna Carta was the first document to control the powers of the monarch and to give some basic freedoms and protection to ordinary people. This is an exaggeration. It did try to control the powers of the monarch, but it mostly benefitted nobles and rich clergy. Perhaps the most important development was the idea that people could not be punished without a trial.

(7) **dyed. To dye** is to change the colour of something using chemicals or plants.

[To dye, dyed, had dyed. Note the difference compared with when a plant or living thing dies: To die, died, had died].

(8) **pillaged** To pillage is to steal and destroy. It is usually used to describe the actions of groups, and sometimes suggests a plan.

For example: *In 455 the Vandals pillaged Rome. The pillaging lasted two weeks.*

There was a riot in the centre of my town last year. Several shops were pillaged and all their contents stolen.

Comprehension

1. What was the problem on the side of the motorway going in the opposite direction?

2. What had Francesca and Pietro done after the family left Gatwick? What else had Pietro done in the car?

3. How did Francesca feel about all the changes in the family's travel plans?

4. What did Pietro say that worried his mother?

5. What was the link between Robin Hood and Lincoln?

6. Who died in Lincoln?

An Exercise in Careful Reading

Francesca likes history and old places so she really wanted to visit Lincoln. The extract above is what she read. Below is what she told her parents and Pietro. She hoped this might make the city more interesting.

How many changes can you identify?

The Lincoln bishops were the richest people in medieval Britain and their estates were the largest and contained more monasteries than the rest of Britain put together. When the nobles and king wrote the Magna Carta in 1215, one of the witnesses was Hugh of Wells, Bishop of Lincoln. The only surviving original of the document is with the records in Lincoln Castle.

In 1141 Lincoln was the site of a battle between King Stephen, the son of William the Conqueror, and the army of Empress Matilda After fierce fighting in the city's streets, Stephen's army was defeated and the king captured.

By 1150, Lincoln was the wealthiest town in England. The basis of the economy was cloth and wool exported to France. Lincoln Cloth, especially the fine clothes died scarlet and green, were famous and the green became even more famous because it was connected with the outlaw Robin Hood who wore Lincoln Green in Sherwood Forest.

Thirteenth-century Lincoln was England's third largest city and a favourite home of several monarchs. It was also home to one of the five main Jewish communities in England

During the First Barons' War, Lincoln was involved in the conflict between the king and rebel barons who had allied with the French. Here, and at Dover, the French and Rebel army was defeated. Lincoln was destroyed because it had supported King Louis of France. In the Second Barons' War of 1266, the rebels attacked the Jews of Lincoln, and badly damaged their synagogue, because they had supported the king.

Answers to the Comprehension

1. There was a long tail back on the motorway going the opposite direction. According to Mrs Pasquati this was at least ten miles long.

2. Both Francesca and Pietro had fallen asleep in the car after they had left Gatwick. Pietro had also taken his shoes off in the car.

3. Francesca was enthusiastic about the changes. *She hated long car journeys when there wasn't an opportunity to stop and explore, and had dreaded the idea of driving all the way from London to Inverness in one day.* She liked the idea of doing the journey in stages and had already identified some places she thought were interesting.

4. Pietro asked why the journey to Lincoln was so slow. He said that he had driven 130 miles in an hour at home.

5. Robin Hood wore Lincoln Green. [Or that was what people said].

6. We don't know the names of the people who died in Lincoln. There was lots of fighting, but the passage does not mention names. King Stephen was not killed there – he was captured. This was a trick question.

The Changes

The Lincoln bishops were the richest people in medieval England and their estates were the largest and contained more monasteries than the rest of **Britain 1 [England was the original. Britain was used in some cases after 1474]** *put together.* **When the nobles and king wrote the 2. [The king did not write this document. He hated it because it limited his powers]** *Magna Carta in 1215, one of the witnesses was Hugh of Wells, Bishop of Lincoln.* **The only surviving original 3. [There are other copies.]** *of the document is with the records in Lincoln Castle.*

In 1141 Lincoln was the site of a battle between King Stephen, **the son 4.[Grandson]** *of William the Conqueror, and the army of Empress Matilda After fierce fighting in the city's streets, Stephen's army was defeated and the king captured.*

By 1150, Lincoln was the wealthiest town in England. The basis of the economy was cloth and wool exported to France **5 [Flanders which is now in modern Belgium].** *Lincoln Cloth, especially the fine clothes died scarlet and green, were famous and the green became even more famous because it was connected with the outlaw Robin Hood who wore Lincoln Green* **in Sherwood Forest. 6 [There is no mention of Sherwood Forest in the original, though tradition says that this is where Robin Hood and his men lived].**

Thirteenth-century Lincoln was England's third largest city and a favourite home of several **monarchs. 7 [The original only mentions kings. Monarchs includes kings and queens].** *It was also home to one of the five main Jewish communities in England*

During the First Barons' War, Lincoln was involved in the conflict between the king and rebel barons who had allied with the French. Here, and at Dover, the French and Rebel army was defeated. Lincoln was **destroyed 8** [Pillages does not mean destroyed. Damaged, but not destroyed] because it had supported **King 9 [Prince]** Louis of France. In the Second Barons' War of 1266, the rebels attacked the Jews of Lincoln, and badly damaged their synagogue, because they had supported the king.

Episode Seventeen

If

If Mr Pasquati had not made a mistake with the family's bookings, they would not have arrived at the wrong airport. If the family had arrived on time, they would not have missed the surprise trip with the MacDonalds, but Francesca would not have enjoyed the long drive north without stops.

And now, as they were driving north on the M11, there were more 'Ifs'. If Pietro had fallen asleep, or played on one of his games, or chatted on his mobile, he would not have seen the large sign on the motorway for **Imperial** (1) **War Museum Duxford.** If Francesca had seen the sign before Pietro she would have tried to distract him (2). But she did not, and he did, and within a few seconds his web search found:

Part of Imperial War Museum Duxford

Mum, Dad can we stop at this Duxford place? It looks really interesting, he asked enthusiastically.

Oh no! Francesca declared. *You are always interested in war and weapons. We've already decided to go to Lincoln. I don't want to change our plans again.*

Pietro laughed. *Almost everything you told us about your Lincoln place involved wars. You just want a bit of history and some shops. Please wonderful, lovely parents. Be kind to your favourite son. We can arrive in this Lincoln place tonight and do it (3) tomorrow.*

Mr Pasquati looked in the car's rear view mirror and laughed. *My favourite son? Do I keep the others in a cupboard? Don't tell your Mum! Is there really a problem Francesca? We can do both things and then you will both be happy. And your Mum will be happy with Lincoln and me with the museum. I am an engineer you know, so this place could be interesting for me. You are an intelligent girl. Please compromise. What can we miss on the way up and then visit on the way back south?*

Francesca paused for a few seconds and then realised that she was being unreasonable. *OK. I'll make a sacrifice for your favourite son. But remember I'm your favourite daughter!* She looked carefully at her map. *If we go straight from Lincoln to Durham we can visit York on the way back. And then go from Durham to Edinburgh and finally Inverness. That works. If you are happy with that, shall I look for hotels?*

Thirty minutes later the family had paid their entrance fee for the museum and were looking at the guides they'd been given. *This place is huge!* Pietro declared. *Look at that Dad! There's everything from really old (4) aircraft to very modern ones.*

The blue plane is an old biplane.(5)

And what about us? Mrs Pasquati asked. Her heart had been set (6) on some shopping in Lincoln that afternoon but she had been keen to please 'the boys' in the family. Mr Pasquati was quite easy going but Pietro had been difficult to please since he became a teenager. *I can't see anything very interesting.*

Sorry dear (7), I wasn't eaves dropping (8) but I heard what you just said. Have you seen the special event we have at present? The speaker was a woman in her late 50s. She was smartly dressed and a large EMMA VOLUNTEER label was pinned to her jacket.

It's a temporary thing. Just until the end of the summer. But we have a section where you can try making biscuits and cakes using ration ingredients from World Wars 1 and 2. It's a bit of a girlie thing, but if you want something more exciting – but quite expensive. We have short flights in some of the old, open cockpit (9) planes. It's very safe, but you need to be happy about being in an open cockpit at 120 MPH (10) and at 3,000 feet. We provide the warm clothes.

Both Mrs Pasquati and Francesca smiled. *I think I'll try the cooking,* Francesca said. *I get travel sick in the car so …..*

Yes, I agree, Mrs Pasquati added quickly. Fortunately, both Enrico and Pietro were out of earshot so the two followed the lady out of the hangar and across the tarmac to another, smaller one.

The family met up again just as the museum was starting to empty at 6. *I actually enjoyed that*, Mrs Pasquati said. There was surprise in her voice. *And look at what we made. Do you want to try it Enrico?*

Mr Pasquati looked cautiously at the biscuits the girls had made, but before he could say anything Pietro took one and immediately announced *Really tasty! You didn't make these did you Fran? Too good for you!*

Actually Pietro, it was your sister who made these. I…. I ate all of mine. That was a very short diet! And Mrs Pasquati laughed.

Yes, I think we all had a good afternoon. Even Pietro, my favourite son, stopped complaining. But we need to make a move. I hate driving in the dark and Lincoln is still a few hours away. Mr Pasquati stopped after a few step. *Does anyone remember where we parked the car?* The rest of the family stopped and looked around with puzzled faces. *Is this even the right car park? Let's split up and search by rows. You all have your mobiles?*

What was the colour and model Enrico? Mrs Pasquati asked. She was clearly worried. *I never take an interest in these things!*

Mr Pasquati paused. *Sorry, I'm not sure. Pietro?*

Unusually for him, Pietro did not have an immediate answer. Then he smiled. *Ring the car rental Dad. You have the registration number and telephone on the car's key and they can tell you the model and colour.*

It took the family nearly half an hour to find their car. *Please tell me that the rest of this holiday is going to be easier,* Mrs Pasquati commented as they turned onto the motorway heading north.

Francesca laughed. *What I find surprising is that it hasn't rained since we arrived. Not what my friends at school told me. And I think this is more exciting than sitting on the beach for two weeks, so let the adventure continue!*

Vocabulary and Culture

The Imperial War Museum at Duxford is Britain's largest aviation museum. It has nearly 200 aircraft in addition to military vehicles, artillery and minor naval vessels in seven main exhibition buildings.

Many visitors say that a full day is required for a visit. The cooking event described here was fictitious, but the museum does organise regular special events.

https://www.iwm.org.uk/visits/iwm-duxford

1. *Imperial* is generally used in British history to describe institutions and system which existed prior to 1947 when India became independent of Britain.
2. *To distract* means to think about something which is of lesser importance at that time.

   For example:

   George had been **distracted** by the idea of watching his favourite football team play that afternoon and forgot to buy the baby's nappies on the way home. His wife was very angry.

   Peter was so **distracted** by the children arguing in the back of the car that he didn't stop at the traffic lights and was fined by the police.

   Helen was so **distracted** by the idea of the exams on Monday that she forgot that she had a date with her boyfriend on Saturday evening.

   Mr Pasquati had been **distracted** by problems at work, which is why he booked the family's flight to the wrong airport.

3. *Do it.* **Informal English**. As used here, the meaning is to visit / to holiday or to explore. So a sentence like *I **did** Spain last year.* would probably mean that the speaker holidayed in Spain the previous year, while *I **did** all the main museums when I was in Rome* would suggest that the speaker had visited all the main museums.
4. Note the use of *really* here to emphasise. *Really* is used in many contexts to emphasise:
   For example:
   I got a ***really*** good mark in my last exam.
   My friend George is ***really*** tall.
   That programme on the T.V. last night was ***really*** boring.
   *Mary is **really** old. She's almost twelve,* said the little girl. [So note that *really* is a personal judgement].

5. *Bi,* meaning two is widely used. For example, ***bifocal*** glasses describes glasses with a combined lens for reading and distance.

In modern English ***bi*** is also used to describe someone who is attracted to both sexes.

UNDERSTAND, BUT BE CAUTIOUS ABOUT HOW, AND WHEN, YOU USE THE TERM.

6. *Her heart had been set on...* That is what she really wanted to do

7. *Sorry dear.* **Informal English.** This is generally used by older women towards younger females and males. **UNDERSTAND, but use** the formal Madam and Sir.

8. *Eaves dropping.*

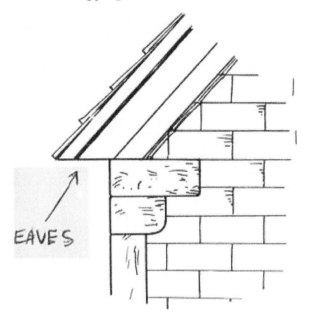

The term comes from a historical time when the walls of most building were *very thin*, so you could stand under the drop of the eaves and listen to the people inside the building.

Perhaps it's not quite so easy now.

This shows the eaves of a house- the intention is that rain flows clear of the wall. In modern houses the rain flows into the gutter which also describes the water collection system on a road.

To end up in the gutter is a term used (especially in the USA?) meaning to be so poor (and perhaps alcoholic or drugged) that you are found lying in the gutter. *If you don't work harder at school, you may end up in the gutter,* is a potential threat from parents.

"HA HA! THEY THINK I'M DRUNK."

9. Cockpit. The place from which the pilot controls a plane. It is now used for old planes and some military aircraft. Large, passenger aircraft have **a flight deck**.

10. MPH Miles per hour.

Comprehension

1. What might have happened if Francesca had been watching the road more carefully?

2. What did Mr Pasquati find amusing?

3. How long did it take to drive to the museum?

4. Why was Mrs Pasquati prepared to change her plan?

5. Where was the cooking event? How had Francesca and Mrs Pasquati learnt about it?

6. Three people seemed surprised by the afternoon? Who were they and why were they surprised?

7. **Using the evidence from this and earlier episodes**, which of the following choices **precisely** describes the family's situation at the museum's parking?

a) They had carefully inspected the larger car which they had collected from Stansted airport.

b) Mr Pasquati knew the exact details of the large car which they had collected from Stansted airport.

c) Mr Pasquati knew what to do and organised the family to hunt for the car.

d) The full details of the car they had collected from Stansted were on the car's key.

e) The family had carefully inspected the larger car which they had exchanged at Stansted airport.

f) None of these.

Answers to the Comprehension

1. If Francesca had been watching the road carefully she might have seen the sign for the museum and diverted Pietro's attention. She wanted to go to Lincoln and not to a war museum.

2. Mr Pasquati found the idea of having *a favourite son* amusing. He had only one son, and Pietro was not always so popular.

3. We don't know the answer to this. Thirty minutes later the family had paid their entrance fee for the museum and were looking at the guides they'd been given. But this does not tell us how long they had been driving.

4. Mrs Pasquati was prepared to change her plans because she wanted to please 'the boys in the family.'

5. Mrs Pasquati and Francesca had learnt about the cooking event from a volunteer called Emma. The event was in a different hangar and Emma had taken them to it.

6. Mrs Pasquati was surprised because she had enjoyed her afternoon. Pietro was surprised because his sister had produced some really tasty biscuits, and Mr Pasquati was surprised that Pietro had enjoyed the afternoon and stopped complaining.

7. **f) None of these.**

Precisely is the key term.

a) They had carefully inspected the larger car which they had collected from Stansted airport.

They implies the family and there is no evidence for this. Mr Pasquati and Pietro had collected the car while the rest of the family had removed the luggage from the earlier, smaller car.

b) Mr Pasquati knew the exact details of the large car which they had collected from Stansted airport.

Sorry, I'm not sure. This was Mr Pasquati's reply when Mrs Pasquati had asked him about the colour and model.

c) Mr Pasquati knew what to do and organised the family to hunt for the car.

It was Pietro who suggested that his father rang the rental company.

d) The full details of the car they had collected from Stansted were on the car's key.

No. Mr Pasquati needed to ring the car rental company to get details of the model and colour.

e) The family had carefully inspected the larger car which they had exchanged at Stansted airport.

If they had carefully inspected the car there would be some knowledge of the colour and model. None of the family knew this.

Some Historical Conditionals

Sorry dear, I wasn't eaves dropping but I heard what you just said. Have you seen the special event we have at present? The speaker was a woman in her late 50s. She was smartly dressed and a large EMMA VOLUNTEER label was pinned to her jacket.

QUESTION

1. What difference would it have made to the afternoon if Emma had not heard the conversation between Mrs Pasquati and Francesca?

It's a temporary thing. Just until the end of the summer. But we have a section where you can try making biscuits and cakes using ration ingredients from World Wars 1 and 2. It's a bit of a girlie thing, but if you want something more exciting – but quite expensive. We have short flights in some of the old, open cockpit (9) planes. It's very safe, but you need to be happy about being in an open cockpit at 120 MPH (10) and at 3,000 feet. We provide the warm clothes.

Questions

1. What would have changed if the Pasquatis had visited the museum on a different time?
2. If Mrs Pasquati or Francesca had chosen to take a flight, what would the museum have provided?

Mr Pasquati looked cautiously at the biscuits the girls had made, but before he could say anything Pietro took one and immediately announced *Really tasty! You didn't make these did you Fran? Too good for you!*

Actually Pietro, it was your sister who made these. I…. I ate all of mine. That was a very short diet! And Mrs Pasquati laughed.

Question

1. What may explain Pietro's reaction to the biscuits?

Yes, I think we all had a good afternoon. Even Pietro, my favourite son, stopped complaining. But we need to make a move. I hate driving in the dark and Lincoln is still a few hours away. Mr Pasquati stopped after a few step. *Does anyone remember where we parked the car?* The rest of the family stopped and looked around with puzzled faces. *Is this even the right car park? Let's split up and search by rows. You all have your mobiles?*

What was the colour and model Enrico? Mrs Pasquati asked. She was clearly worried. *I never take an interest in these things!*

Mr Pasquati paused. *Sorry, I'm not sure. Pietro?*

Unusually for him, Pietro did not have an immediate answer. Then he smiled. *Ring the car rental Dad. You have the registration number and telephone on the car's key and they can tell you the model and colour.*

It took the family nearly half an hour to find their car. *Please tell me that the rest of this holiday is going to be easier,* Mrs Pasquati commented as they turned onto the motorway heading north.

Question

What would have happened if Pietro had not had [hadn't had] the idea of ringing the car hire company?

Answers

What difference would it have made to the afternoon if Emma had not heard the conversation between Mrs Pasquati and Francesca?

If Emma **had not heard** their conversation, Mrs Pasquati and Francesca **would have not gone to** [would have missed] the special event.

What would have changed if the Pasquatis had visited the museum on a different date?

If the Pasquatis **had visited** the museum on a different date **they might have missed** the special event because it was temporary. [Note that **might** is uncertain. A possibility]

If Mrs Pasquati or Francesca had chosen to take a flight, what would the museum have provided?

If they had taken a flight, the museum **would have provided** warm clothes.

What may explain Pietro's reaction to the biscuits?

If Pietro had tried Francesca's biscuits before **he would have known** the quality of her biscuits.

What would have happened if Pietro had not had [hadn't had] the idea of ringing the car hire company?

If Pietro hadn't had the idea of ringing the car hire company the family **would have spent*** many hours looking for their car.

*To check. You know the idea of spending time? [To spend/ spent/spent].

I usually spend Sunday lunch time with my parents but May normally spends her Sunday with her grandparents.

I spent yesterday evening watching television.

My brother **came** home early from his trip to Germany because **he had spent** all his travel money.

A Final Check

The section below, which is based on the story, contains nine mistakes. Some are mistakes of grammar, some of spelling and some of facts. How many can you find?

You will need to read carefully and you may need to re-read some of the storey.

....

The Pasquatis had had many problems on their way to Scotland. The first day had started badly because Mrs Pasquati had left her passport at the office and then they been delayed by traffic on the motorway.

There had even been problems the night before because Mr Pasquati's business meeting had not been totally successful. The contract he had been looking forward to had not been signed. Francesca had also been difficult because she suddenly decided she wanted a dress her mother packed in a suitcase.

To make things worse, at the airport the family discovered that Mr Pasquati had made a mistake in their flights. He usually travelled to Gatwick for business. As a result the family had a flight for Gatwick Airport south of London, though they actually wanted to go to Stansted Airport which is north of London. Pietro realised this when they were in the café at the airport, but they already missed their flight and landed at Gatwick late in the day.

The next problem was that the car Mr Pasquati booked was at Stansted and when they went to the car hire at Gatwick they didn't have a large car. Mr Pasquati wanted a large vehicle for their long drive north. In the meantime, their Scottish friends were upset because they had booked a special trip to Edinburgh.

But then things started to improve. The car hire company ringed Mr Pasquati to tell him that they now had a car for him at Stansted, and the family spend most of the afternoon doing different things at a museum near Cambridge. There was a final hiccup when they discovered they had forgotten where they parked the car but that problem was resolved when resolved when Pietro *had a bright idea** and suggested they ring the care hire company to get the car's details. We close this part of the story with the family driving happily north, the rest of their adventure before them

A Final Check

You will need to read carefully and you may need to re-read some of the **storey.**

DID YOU REMEMBER THAT ONE? You met it earlier. STORY IN A BOOK. STOREY IN A BUILDING.

The Pasquatis had had many problems on their way to Scotland. The first day had started badly because **Mrs Pasquati [It was Mr Pasquati]** had left her **HIS** passport at the office and **then they had been delayed** by traffic on the motorway.

There had even been problems the night before because Mr Pasquati's business meeting had not been totally successful. The contract he had been looking forward to had not been signed. Francesca had also been difficult because she suddenly decided she wanted a dress her mother **had** packed in a suitcase.

To make things worse, at the airport the family discovered that Mr Pasquati had made a mistake **with** their flights. He usually travelled to Gatwick for business. As a result the family had a flight for Gatwick Airport south of London, though they actually wanted to go to Stansted Airport which is north of London. **Pietro realised this when they were in** the café at the airport, but they **had** already missed their flight and landed at Gatwick late in the day. **[It was the stranger in the café who saw that they had missed their flight.]**

The next problem was that the car Mr Pasquati booked was at Stansted, and when they went to the car hire at Gatwick they didn't have a large car. Mr Pasquati wanted a large vehicle for their long drive north. In the meantime, their Scottish friends were upset because they had booked a special trip to Edinburgh. **[No, it was to the Orkneys.]**

But then things started to improve. The car hire company **rang** Mr Pasquati to tell him that they now had a car for him at Stansted, and the family **spent** most of the afternoon doing different things at a museum near Cambridge. There was a final hiccup when they discovered they had forgotten where they **had** parked the car, but that problem was resolved when resolved when Pietro *had a bright idea** and suggested they ring the care hire company to get the car's details. We close this part of the story with the family driving happily north, the rest of their adventure before them. **Missed the full stop.**

In some exams this results in a .5% grade reduction for each error.

had a bright idea* Made an intelligent suggestion to solve a problem.

The second book in Progressing in English

The Pasquatis Discover East Anglia ©

will be available in late 2021 and will introduce new grammar and vocabulary as we follow the Pasquatis on their journey north.

Printed in Great Britain
by Amazon